Strings to my Bow

Strings to my Bow

a memoir

Watson Forbes

StarNine

Published in UK by StarNine Design Print.
Registered Office: The Coach House, Great Wolford, WARKS CV36 5NQ

Printed and Bound in Great Britain by The Alden Press, Oxford, UK.

A Catalogue record for this book is available from the British Library.

ISBN 0 9524752 0 0

*Photograph of William Primrose reproduced
By Courtesy of The Primrose International Viola Archive at Brigham Young University. UTAH. USA.*

*Articles on the Viola Repertoire
reprinted By Courtesy of 'The Strad' Magazine.*

Cover Illustration by James Ibbotson

Contents

5.   Foreword

9.   Early Life

20.   Learning to Play

31.   Thoughts on Art

36.   Entering the Music Profession

46.   Quartet Playing

57.   The War Years — and after

64.   Solo Playing and Teaching

73.   Violas and Viola Players

79.   Head of Music, BBC Scotland

95.   Retiring from the BBC

108.   Hobbies

112.   Coda

116.   *Appendix One*
An analysis of the Viola Repertoire
in articles written originally for
"The Strad" Magazine

173.   *Appendix Two*
The Principle of "Arrangements"

175.   *Appendix Three*

Complete Catalogue of
published Arrangements

FOREWORD

In September 1926 Watson Forbes and I met for the first time. Barely 17 years of age, and brought up in ancient towns in the east of Scotland, we found ourselves lodging in London with a number of young men and women, most of whom were students across the road at the Royal Academy of Music. This was the beginning of a friendship that has been cherished for well over 60 years.

Two periods are specially close in my memory. There were the exciting years after the war when so much was stirring in London. Watson was to be centrally involved in it all: the Aeolian String Quartet, London String Trio, London Piano Quartet, a Duo with the pianist Alan Richardson, and more. His influence was unmistakable, and it extended through teaching and writing.

Many years later he became Head of Music at the BBC in Glasgow, an inspired appointment which all who passed that way remember with admiration and affection. He also found time for chamber music with members of the BBC Scottish Symphony Orchestra and with his wife Jean, and to establish a delightful Arts Festival in Montrose, not far from where we started. I look forward very much to reading this book, which will bring back so many happy memories.

Robin Orr

Cambridge 1993

Chapter 1

Early Life

'Are you in earnest? Seize this very minute;
What you can do, or dream you can, begin it;
Boldness has genius, power, and magic in it.
Only engage, and then the mind grows heated;
Begin, and then the work will be completed.'
                                                    Goethe

When my friends used to ask me what were my three great loves in life, I would answer, 'Wine, women and string quartets'; but the real passion of my life has been — and still is — the strains of the violin (although, eventually, circumstances dictated that I should be a viola player).

St Andrews where I was born in 1909, is a small but remarkable place: a cathedral city (though the cathedral is in ruins), the home of golf and dominated by the Royal & Ancient Club, it also holds a university which is the oldest foundation of learning in Scotland. I spent the first sixteen years of my life there. My parents were industrious and very proud of their jeweller's shop. My mother had the business brain, and my father the flair. Cultural activity in St Andrews was minimal in spite of the presence of the university, and of the most basic sort, largely influenced by the Scottish folk music tradition and the popular songs of the day. A few enlightened enthusiasts did their best to add a modicum of culture to life, but their efforts were rarely appreciated.

My father was a modest amateur violinist and hearing him play was a great joy to me. I fell in love with the sound of the violin and received my first lessons from him when I was five years old. Later I had lessons with local teachers, and eventually went weekly to Dundee for my tuition, to

H. Everitt Loseby for violin, and to James Hinchcliffe for piano. Somehow, out of very limited means, my mother found the money and guidance for my early days. She, though not musical, was a stickler for practice; I resisted but she usually won, and the ensuing tears which fell upon my long suffering violin are there to this day to testify to the battles we waged. Despite discouragement at school, it was through my mother's tenacity that I found my way into the musical profession.

My mother was one of numerous children - I think the eldest girl. Her mother was Scottish, coming from East Lothian; her father came from Liverpool but settled in North Berwick for a while. She received the basic Scottish education, leaving school as soon as possible to take up a variety of jobs to help with the family fortunes, finally ending up in a jeweller's shop.

My father came from Montrose and was one of several children. His father had been an adventurous lad, running away from school and going off to sea as a cabin boy while still quite young. He returned to land to study seamanship, then went off once more to serve before the mast on a sailing schooner. Later he returned again to gain his Master's certificate — he was obviously a man of great determination. He finally became captain of his vessel and made several successful voyages to the West Indies.

He retired from the sea early and bought a row of houses in which he invested his hard won earnings, but unfortunately these proved to be hardly enough for his needs, and the First World War brought him into financial straits. After this he lived a very restricted life looked after by his three daughters.

His wife, my grandmother, died young, leaving my grandfather a widower in his declining years. He was a great, very sturdy man with a voice like a foghorn. I can well believe the story of how, at Archangel, his ship being held captive by the ice-flows, he used to have the ice broken and each member of his crew lowered by rope for a dip in the icy water. They survived! Furthermore, he lost no member of his crew in the prevailing arctic conditions, which was more than could be said of most seamen stranded in port.

My memory of him is somewhat dim, but I do recall one

incident. When I arrived hungry and slightly tearful after the long journey north by train, his turned to his daughters and commanded 'For the love of God, fill the bairn's kite' (stomach)!

My father left school early to become apprenticed to a local Montrose jeweller and after a year or two he left to take up a similar position as assistant to a jeweller in Galashiels. There, he shared digs with the local organist, who did much to foster his love of music and certainly improved his fiddling, and there too, he met my mother who fell in love with his bright red hair. Thoughts of married bliss received no encouragement from either side of the family so they eloped and were married at an Edinburgh Registry Office. The fact that they eloped was typical of my mother; deeds not creeds seems to have been her motto. Together they settled in St Andrews and set up business with capital borrowed from the family; they had a struggle to keep going, but keep going they did.

Sixty years later we had a great celebration for their diamond wedding, in Glasgow. They also got a telegram of congratulation from Her Majesty the Queen. My father wondered how the Queen could have known, so I said to him - 'Well, Dad, it's quite simple. When Philip woke up this morning and saw the date, he nudged the Queen and said - 'Look, Elizabeth, we mustn't forget, we've got to send a telegram to David and Isabella Forbes, it's their diamond wedding today'.' My father was still completely mystified, and whether or not he believed me I cannot say but, having a slightly fey imagination, he may well have done. My mother made no comment but inwardly she was very pleased - even delighted.

The commencement of the First World War was a distinct blow especially as my father was presently called up to serve in the army. He never struck me as having particularly good health, but the medical board who examined him must have been very much up to the mark for he lived until he was ninety-two! So my parents were faced with a dilemma, either to close down the business or struggle to survive; my mother determined on the latter course, which naturally placed a heavy burden on her shoulders; it was a formidable task but somehow she managed to keep the business going through the trying years. She had business acumen, grit and determination, and withal a sweetness of nature to lighten the burden. She was generous to a fault. In my wife Jean's words, she was the perfect mother-in-law. She had only one failing - she never learnt how to receive.

My father was not a distinguished soldier, he was neither aggressive nor foolhardy - not the stuff that heroes are made of - although when I was a little boy he was a hero in my eyes. He brought home many entertaining tales of his experiences in France, but how true they were I could never fathom. I cannot honestly say that he told lies, but his version of an episode was so embroidered with fantastic detail as to have little relation to the actual happening. For instance, before the last offensive which was to bring us actual victory, his siege gun battery was ordered to withdraw some distance behind the line. So the battery shouldn't be annihilated by a stray bomb, the men were dispatched two by two and my father, together with the cook, were to be the last to leave. Over a makeshift fire the cook placed a sheet of corrugated iron and proceeded to fry the remaining eggs for the departing troops. My father started eating the eggs as they became available, and actually consumed eleven fried eggs before his turn came to depart; he was so full of beans (or eggs) when his turn came, that he ran the race of his life and was the first of his battery to arrive at the focal point of assembly!

Before going to France he did a spell of guard duty on Beachy Head, his period of duty being from 2.00 to 4.00 am. He was told to walk back and forth in front of a sentry box, and, as the night was slightly foggy, before long he lost his bearings (sense of direction was never his strong point, his wife was always losing him!) and started floundering about trying to find the box. Soon he realised he was lost and that Beachy Head, noted for its number of suicides, was not the place to be wandering about in the pitch dark. So, having at last bumped into the box, he thankfully retired inside and stayed there smoking cigarettes for the rest of his duty (fortunately, the UK was not invaded that night).

He was a gentle soul, not without a canny sense of humour. I once asked him if he had come across any Germans while he was in France; no, he hadn't. What would he had done if he had encountered any? "Run like Hell!" He was artistic, even in his hand-writing, which had a most individual touch; his drawings, even in old age, had a fine liveliness of spirit. He loved his home in Hendon, and adored his flat in Glasgow. Some of his happiest experiences were his attendance at the public concerts of the BBC Scottish Symphony Orchestra in the Glasgow Studio; how he revelled in the technical accomplishment of the various soloists. He always sat beside me in the front row and was inordinately proud of my position as Head of Music for Scotland.

Some years later, after I had retired from the BBC and we were all living in Loch Goil, he died peacefully in his bed after a good glass of sherry. He was ninety-two.

I was destined to be an only child, not a situation I can recommend, though it had its advantages. I was five years old when the First World War broke out and, oddly enough, I can remember the occasion, just one of those odd quirks of memory. I went to a fee-paying school, the Madras College in St Andrews, so called because the founder had made his fortune in Madras. As schools go I suppose it was reasonably good, though I cannot say that I was very happy there; nor did I gain anything but a very basic education; music and the arts were generally frowned upon. My chief delights were when our history master played us records of actors declaiming speeches from Shakespeare, and our English mistress would read us excerpts from Kipling and Robert Louis Stevenson. Some years later when I was adjudicating at the Edinburgh Competitive Music Festival, a group was entered from my old school and they were very good, good enough to come first in their class—how things must have changed!

We had some distinguished lads in my class. One was the son of the maths teacher who was quite brilliant at maths, so much so that I was most astonished when, at the end of the year, he got the prize for music, and I the prize for maths! I lay no claim to being in any way distinguished, but the other chap went on to be knighted for his services in Egypt— Sir John Carmichael.

Between the ages of ten and fourteen I spent some of the summer holidays in the country with my maternal grandparents. My grandfather worked on a farm in charge of two cart horses called Prince and Punch. My grandmother was a dutiful, if somewhat imperious wife who had

13

produced nine, ten, or even eleven children—she was always rather vague about the number! They inhabited a primitive, lonely cottage, with no running water and only make-shift sanitation. We drew water in pails from a pump in the woods several times a day. The change from my home life was pretty horrendous but not without its compensations. It was a complete change from town to country life and I was to learn of a different kind of 'hard labour', for my grandfather's life represented continuous hard work, seven days a week, year in year out. He was slow moving, taking his pace from the changing seasons, but nonetheless achieving a great deal. Nature never seems to hurry—nor did he. He lived close to the earth, and was not insensitive to the beauties of nature, having in his care bees, hens, sheep and cows, the care of hay, fruit and vegetables, and the work of the forests. His independence was affected by the tranquil yet rugged nature of his surroundings, so that he acquired a stature, a strength of character, and a fine dignity of mien. He was an upright, as well as a kindly and loveable man who realised that he was dealing with the original calling of mankind and that much depended on his husbandry and good fortune. Such was my grandfather. Nothing gave me greater pleasure than to go off with him at break of day, driving the two great horses in tandem, returning at dusk, hungry and tired but fulfilled.

I never stayed long enough to gain anything but a superficial idea of country life, in spite of the fact that I went hay making, fetched coal for the big house, helped to fell trees in the forest, worked with the sheep dog controlling the sheep, milked the cows—what endless variety. Then there were the more domestic jobs like feeding the hens, picking apples and gooseberries (a most painful task!) and red, white and black currants; there was even fishing in the stream, though this was not often very rewarding.

I had my violin with me, though with so many distractions practising was rather spasmodic. It was a lonely life for a boy of my age and there was little encouragement towards music-making. However, I did make contact with one old amateur with whom I played duets—including some difficult ones by Spohr which must have sounded ghastly; however, we enjoyed our efforts.

One time, passing through Edinburgh, I strayed with my

father around the barrows of second-hand books at the top of Leith Walk; there I discovered a volume of the six unaccompanied Violin Sonatas and Partitas by Bach, all for sixpence—a penny each! What a bargain. When I changed over to the viola it continued to be my almost daily practice. I still have the volume. It has been my constant companion for over seventy years. What a treasure, what a glorious find—and all so cheap, which gladdens my Scottish heart!

Practising has always been a bit of a chore, something to be got through somehow. When I first started to play the violin, aged five, I played my father's repertoire. He played with me most of the time through the violin tutor of Berthold Tours and another book of studies by one whose name I doubtfully recall was Henry Farmer. I soon outplayed my father to such an extent that I was sent to have lessons with the local teacher who distinguished herself playing at the local cinema for 'the pictures'.

My mother was thorough and insisted that I learn about the theory of music, so my violin teacher's husband was roped in to give me lessons in the rudiments of music. These interested me greatly, and I recall wading through Macpherson's Rudiments of Music and even some of the earlier chapters of his book on harmony. Incidentally, when writing music, I still make the treble clef as I was taught then, and in fact my clear music penmanship stems from this early tuition. He also encouraged me to buy a three-volume book by Scholes about the great composers and an encyclopaedia by Dunstan—these are still in use.

I practised and played (don't ever confuse the two activities) in the sitting room and in the room behind the shop. In the latter place I had to stop when anyone came into the shop. I played the *Souvenir* by Dradla, the *Henry Vlll Dances* by Edward German, concertos by De Beriot and Oscar Reiding and eventually some of the easier pieces by Kreisler. Great fun—though disconcerting when I had the piano accompaniments played with me. The *'Star Folios'* were a great stand-by. Somehow we acquired a piano by Reisbach and I graduated on to a larger violin than the half-size outfit I started on. Music at school was frowned upon, though I vaguely remember having a period in a small orchestra playing a second violin part.

I found time for music at the beginning and end of the

day. I was roused by my father at 7.00 am and practised piano and violin for a hour before going off to school at 9.00 am. I had another hour of music before going to bed. I slowly progressed so that my local teacher could no longer teach me and it was then, when I was about eleven years old, that I went to Dundee on a Saturday to have lessons in both violin and piano. Highlights were concerts in the Caird Hall by Kreisler and Heifetz. I remember Kreisler played the Mendelssohn concerto with piano accompaniment played by Charlton Keith; he left the stage after the first movement, thereby ignoring Mendelssohn's instructions for a continuous performance with links between the movements. I enjoyed those concerts and resolved to do better and better. I was religious in those days, so that I prayed for God to make me the best violinist in Scotland.

While my father was away winning the war, my mother and I kept the home fires burning. As an occasional treat we would go to the cinema to see yet another episode of Pearl White in *The Hooded Terror* and sometimes as a real treat we had fish and chips from the local frying shop.

I inherited from my parents—and also from my maternal grandmother—a deep regard for superstition which haunted my entire youth. This accompanied my belief in religion, a particular kind of rather severe Presbyterianism favoured by East Coast Scotland at the beginning of the century. The superstition took the form of omens of doom and disaster, only occasionally regarding the pleasanter aspects of coming events. These omens were found in lines in the palms of the hands, various kinds of horoscopes and such mundane ideas as the setting of the tea-leaves after draining a cup of tea; black cats coming up one's path, and (a sure signal for death in the family) the vase of white flowers in the sitting room! Religion, too, was largely primitive; a recording angel hovered over my head, duly writing down in a book the good and bad things I did during each day—even to noting the bad thoughts I had indulged in. This book was to be produced and inspected on the day of judgement and, according to the weight of evidence, I would be confined to hell or elevated to the joys of paradise! God and the Devil were very much in evidence.

What seems so remarkable in retrospect is that I was swayed in my attitude to life by these ideas; they plagued my existence to such an extent that unhappiness and a sense of impending doom were my constant companions. What is even more remarkable is the fact that I was cured of these beliefs by chance remarks from colleagues, just as suddenly and completely as I had earlier given up my belief in Santa Claus.

I abandoned superstition when I was seventeen or eighteen, and my religious beliefs and practices when I was twenty—both quite suddenly and completely. I have never returned to either; in fact, I felt like Christian in Bunyan's Pilgrim's Progress when the burden fell from his shoulders—a feeling of relief, not unmingled with apprehension as to what might befall me pervaded my whole being. I entered a new phase where philosophy became my way of life. Organised Christianity as exemplified by the Church was abandoned; God was replaced by nature; prayer by contemplation.

I read an astounding number and variety of books from the early Greeks to the modern philosophers, never becoming too deeply involved but endeavouring to keep the simple attitude to life's problems. Then I encountered Humanism, and was satisfied to have found what I was seeking.

On the whole I have had a very fortunate life; good luck came to me quite early on and has since smiled on me in all my undertakings. I was only twelve years old when I made up my mind to be a musician—to be a violinist. I had appeared with great success in Dundee at the 'end of year concert', and that had gone to my head (though I have to admit that my real thrill was wearing my new yellow stockings with red garters!) A successful appearance at the Perth Musical Festival soon afterwards finally convinced me. In all these decisions I had the full backing of my parents although it was a complete reversal of their previous plans. Being in St Andrews, a university town, I had been destined to become a Minister—a parson. All their future hopes were centred in me as I was an only child. Most of my friends were destined for a university career. It must have been a real blow to my parents when I announced my decision to plough a lonely and individual course. Neither of them knew much, if anything, about musical education, but somehow or other they made the correct moves and obtained the best music teachers in our locality. The upshot was that a the age of sixteen I entered the Royal Academy of Music in London.

During my studentship I returned occasionally to Scotland to see my parents and my grandmother who lived with them after the death of my grandfather. Tired and sleepy, I was confounded the first morning of one visit to behold my grandmother—then in her seventies—bringing me a cup of tea while I was still in bed (it should have been the other way around). However, I ventured a remark somewhat sheepishly, 'There's' nothing like a cup of tea first thing in the morning', to which she replied, 'Aye, it girs aw the wee doors to open'.

When I was a child I was taught to hate the French—a nasty untrustworthy nation; later, as the First World War started, I was taught to hate the Germans—a nasty, brutal nation; after that war it was the Russians—a nasty, over-ambitious nation, full of communists; and, being Scottish, I was naturally at daggers drawn with the English.

To travel abroad is an education, and for me it has been the source of enlightening and beneficial experiences. The French treated me with kindness and, even after the ghastly war of 1939-1945, the Germans were most kind, considerate and helpful. With the Russians I had only occasional contacts, and those were always friendly. As for the English, I made my home and my career amongst them for the greater part of my life, and was most happy to be there. During one brief spell I returned to Scotland and was amazed to find the old animosity still rampant. Hate is insidious; it eats into one's imagination and becomes rank and self-destroying. Why was such hate generated in the first place? Every Sunday as a young lad I attended church, and listened to Christ's admonitions to love one's neighbour and to love one's enemies. It had little effect, or so it seemed. But it has, since then, given me pause for much thought.

The fact that I am an only-child, and not given to belonging, willingly, to crowds, saved me from the worst influences of hate; my hate was nationalistic, but it side-stepped that passionate conviction which, at its worst, leads to war. When war broke out in 1939 I volunteered for air-raid service and, later, joined the RAF as a musician, where I remained as a member of the RAF Symphony

Orchestra and most fortunately never saw active service.

Advancing age has brought with it a more tolerant attitude, but although my hate may have lessened, a profound dislike of social injustice remains.

Chapter 2

Learning to Play

I entered the Royal Academy of Music in 1926 as a violinist, a rather raw lad of sixteen, and left six years later as a viola player, more by accident than design.

My career as a student was rather chequered in as much as I had a great variety of professors. I was first scheduled to have lessons with M. Wessely, but unfortunately he died during the summer before I came south to the RAM. I was seconded to Sydney Robjohns with whom I stayed very briefly. He had very little to impart to me, being over sympathetic and lacking in precision of method. I then had Edith Knocker who had been assistant to Leopold Auer in Russia and she brought me on quite a bit. I studied many of the Kreisler pieces with her as well as some of the classics of violin literature. She laid a good foundation to my technique and taught me style in fiddling. I stayed with her quite a few terms and progressed well.

After Edith Knocker retired I had a few lessons from Paul Beard which were not very satisfactory from my point of view. He gave me Paganini and difficult pieces to practise which were beyond my powers but gave me no tips about how to tackle these works and so I was left to my own devices which were not equal to the task. However, I managed to get transferred to Marjorie Hayward and settled down to some real productive work. She found my interpretations 'straight-laced' but failed to acquaint me with tempo rubato. She did, however drill me in many basic ideas, and these I found most helpful.

I found the burden of examinations a frightful bore, interrupting one's studies to become a musician. I still think they are an unnecessary nuisance, but the majority of students seemed to find them useful as an indication of their progress, and so the examinations remain.

I enjoyed the orchestra, particularly when it was conducted by Sir Henry Wood. Sir Henry was a great inspiration; as soon as he entered the Academy the whole place seemed to leap into life and take on a new tempo. I enjoyed his rehearsals. From my audition I was placed principal second violin; in time I transferred to the first violins, and eventually ended up by sharing the first desk with Vivian Dunn (later knighted for his services to military music).

While the violin and cello sections of the orchestra were fully manned by students, the other string sections and the wind and brass were led by imported professionals—mostly professors at the Academy whose pupils benefited from additional tuition in the orchestral repertoire. The oboist Leon Goossens was the outstanding coach—surrounded by an adoring gallery of female students—and many were the times I admired his lovely tone and expert handling of the solos.

The repertoire was pretty comprehensive, including as it did most of the major symphonic works, a goodly selection of arias and concertos sung and played by students, and Sir Henry's arrangements of excerpts from the classical repertoire, especially from Wagner's operas. I particularly recall his meticulous care over Beethoven's 9th Symphony and his sympathetic accompaniments to the various concertos which were presented for rehearsal. But I especially remember his preparation of the St Matthew Passion of Bach to which he devoted endless trouble and gave, eventually, a most memorable performance in the Queen's Hall. He conducted the student rehearsals with the same quick but thorough detail he expended on the preparation for the annual Promenade Concerts. Indeed, many of the students found their way into the profession by joining the Queen's Hall Orchestra. *

I shall always feel grateful to him for his inspiration at these afternoon rehearsals, and for all I learnt about orchestral repertoire and orchestral discipline from this truly great man. One felt that Sir Henry was the gateway into the profession and it was he who caused me to change my intention of becoming a good teacher into one of becoming a member of an orchestra, and a professional violinist.

A selection of players would be chosen to play for the yearly opera performance which was given at the Scala Theatre. I took part in several of these, and I particularly remember one which was elaborately staged and thoroughly rehearsed—Wagner's *Die Meistersinger*. It was a terrifying experience; we hardly had room to draw a full bow, the orchestral pit was so cramped for room. Some of the singers performed well, but others obviously felt that singing such taxing music in a large theatre placed a strain on their voices. If the experiment was regarded as a success, it was one which was not to be repeated; shortly thereafter the Academy was extended and housed a small theatre for more suitable operas, chosen with the students in mind.

At first I had no tuition in ensemble work, having left Lionel Tertis very unimpressed with my playing. He was in full control of chamber music during my time as a student and it was not until much later that I discovered that Herbert Withers was also teaching ensemble work and joined his class. I must have made some progress as I was called by Tertis to apply for the position of second violin in Sidney Griller's quartet. I didn't get the position, which was just as well as I was not yet fit for it.

I started appearing at 'Fortnightly Concerts' with some success and became a member of the string quartet which gradually became the premier ensemble in the RAM. The members were David Carl Taylor and myself, violins, Gwynne Edwards, viola, and David Ffrancon Thomas cello. The quartet was allowed to take outside engagements, and played at Cambridge University and even at No. 11 Downing Street. The ensemble was awarded the Sir Edward Cooper and RAM Club Prizes for quartet playing at the Academy in 1929 and 1930.

We played a good mixture of classical and romantic music. Our only blemish was a poor rendering of Mozart's D major quartet (K499)—a work I never enjoyed, even later in life. We were intoxicated by the sensuous beauty of the Ravel quartet and gave some spirited performances of the *Biscay* quartet by Sir J. B. McEwen, then Principal at the Academy

A quartet doesn't run itself; it requires organising. The experience gained as a student stood me in very good stead in years to come. I undertook much of the chore of arranging rehearsals and venues, writing to people and, most importantly, getting the music we were to play. I started buying music whenever I could afford it, a practice carried over into my professional life so that over the years I have been able to build up a fine library of chamber music.

We thoroughly enjoyed our lessons with Herbert Withers who instilled in us a great love of chamber music and a love of the string quartet, and I will always be grateful to him for his enthusiasm. It was he who persuaded me to take up the viola, which I did at first very reluctantly until I played York Bowen's first sonata at an Academy concert and enjoyed a greater success than I had ever had on the violin. As Herbert Withers truly said, 'As a viola player, you will never be without a job'. Then, still as a violinist, I won a Sir James Caird Scholarship and spent the following summer in Pisek, Czechoslovakia studying with Sevcík. I had been introduced to Sevcík exercises by Marjorie Hayward, a former Sevcík pupil, and to receive lessons from the great man himself was most stimulating. Under his guidance I studied and played some of the most difficult works for the violin, chiefly because he showed me how to tackle them. Music thus became my settled and complete study with every note in place. In my enthusiasm I found myself getting up at about 5 a.m. and practising for two hours before breakfast; then three hours between breakfast and lunch. The afternoons were spent in recreation along the banks of the river following Sevcík to his special eyrie erected by the municipality where he elaborated on his method. Then more practice after tea, followed by a get-together with Sevcík around the table in the hotel for a chat about fiddlers and fiddling.

Returning to England, I still played the violin but also practised the viola. I changed from Marjorie Hayward to Raymond Jeremy as my professor and gradually eased my way into the profession as a viola player. Raymond Jeremy was a most sympathetic teacher and I am so grateful to him for all the help he gave me. He had a distinguished career as a quartet player, taking part in the first performances, given under the composer's direction, of Elgar's String Quartet and Piano Quintet at the Wigmore Hall in 1919, with Albert Sammons and W. H. Reed (violins), the cellist Felix Salmond and the pianist William Murdoch.

I had a few lessons with Rowsby Woof in the hope that he would improve my vibrato—alas with little effect—and later I had some inspired lessons from that great violinist Albert Sammons.

How we tend to underestimate our great men. It's quite disgraceful. Sammons was one of the world's great violinists and a most loveable man! His performances of the Elgar and Delius violin concertos were magnificent, yet he remained a modest artist, bubbling over with ideas, especially when he was teaching. From him I learnt how to perform; I learnt which fingering and bowing was most likely to come off under the stress of public performance. But, more than that, it was never a case of playing a piece for one's own edification or enjoyment, it was the reaction of the audience which counted. It was no use being emotionally involved with the music if the audience remained aloof. How to communicate with an audience was what he showed me, and I was ever grateful to him for explaining and demonstrating the difference in attitude.

At the time of my lessons with Sammons I was in the midst of changing from violin to viola. When I turned up for a lesson with my viola, playing some of the unaccompanied Bach movements, he took it in his stride and was wonderfully helpful. Of course I studied the Elgar and Delius concertos with him, playing the violin. Sammons recommended I have some lessons with Lionel Tertis, but these were not very successful.

So far as the Delius concerto was concerned, he showed me what Delius had originally written and what he, Sammons, had substituted by way of technical display—to the obvious advantage of the work. There was always a period in each lesson during which we would just chat about music, or about the profession and concert giving. Once he told me of an amusing incident. Because of bad weather and poor train service, he and his accompanist arrived late at a girls' school to give a recital. As they arrived, they were welcomed by the music mistress who took them straight to the hall, where they were greeted by the girls all standing up as they made their way to the artist's room at the back of the platform. They soon discovered that the only facilities for a wash and brush up were through the hall at the other end of the building. So through the hall they had to parade again, and all the girls stood up once more After a hasty toilet they again went through the hall and once more, the girls stood up in greeting. This, eventually, was too much even for the well regimented girls, and as the players approached the artist's room they gave the luckless musicians a round of applause!

At the Academy I was lucky in that my composition professor was Theodore Holland, a slow-moving man in his sixties when I knew him. He had a friend, a fellow professor, equally deliberate in his movements We christened them 'pas vite' and 'non troppo'. He probably realised that I had little talent for original composition and was thus delighted to help me with my viola arrangements.

I am grateful to him for his encouragement and for the firm foundation he laid, but I am also grateful to him in another respect for he wrote a Suite for me and kindly invited me to his house week after week to try out his ideas in various forms. It was my first chance to work with a composer and I learnt a great deal about how to write for viola and piano during these weekly encounters—how to find the best register for melodies and passage work, how easy it is to drown the viola by a piano part which lies in the same register as the viola, how it is possible to write effectively quite high up on the A string provided it is well supported by the piano, and, especially, what a treasure it is that violas have in the C string. Alas, I lost touch with the Theodore Holland Suite, but I would love to peruse it once again, if only to revive memories of all the diligent, exploratory times we enjoyed together.

In the years that have followed I have had the pleasure of working with many composers in the preparation of their works for performance and have found some more helpful than others. Discussions about tempo and expression are often useful and interesting, but in matters of actual performance—the presentation of a work to an audience— I have found the composer sometimes ill-equipped to give advice. Creation is one activity; presentation and performance, especially in the realisation of what is possible and what is acceptable—quite a different matter. When a performer is preparing a work he must first of all, after gleaning the general idea of the music, work on its technical aspects; then, having overcome these difficulties, he is ready to play the music for his own satisfaction and enjoyment, but chiefly for his own realisation of the musical purpose of the work. Finally, and this is the stage which is often neglected, he must prepare the music for performance to an audience. The purpose is to make the audience feel the purport of the music as he himself felt it when he was playing it through for his own enjoyment—it is the audience who are to be affected, not the performer. Technical modifications may have to be incorporated; emotional stress limited, but projected; tempi revised for better understanding. And it is often at this point that composer and performer are at loggerheads, each failing to understand that it is the work itself that is important.

It was during this time at the Academy that I had my first audition and played as a violinist. The examining body were quite impressed but had no vacancy in the New Symphony Orchestra. However, they were delighted to hear that I also played the viola. Imagine my surprise and gratification when I received an invitation to play the viola at their next concert. My gratification was slightly marred when, to my chagrin, I discovered that I had to read the difficult viola part of Beethoven's *Coriolan* overture at rehearsal, and found my reading of the alto clef sadly at fault. However, I eventually memorised the part and all went off satisfactorily.

How brave my parents were to send me from a small remote city in Scotland to the vastness of London. How they managed to afford it all I shall never discover. They paid for everything, my tuition, my lodging and even gave me pocket money in addition. I was lucky to be housed in a students' hostel where I met some interesting young musicians. One of these, Robin Orr, who was studying the organ at the Royal College of Music, astonished me by moving on to Cambridge University to study music. I considered this to be an unwise move. As he went on to become a lecturer at Cambridge, then a professor at Glasgow University, and later returned to Cambridge as Professor of Music, I was obviously wrong! My sole ambition was to become a player and performer. I scorned the academic side of music. How little I knew of the music profession and of its wide possibilities at that time.

I also had as a welcome colleague the pianist and

composer Alan Richardson, with whom I eventually joined up as a duo and we enjoyed many successful years together. He encouraged me in my arrangements and we published many of these together before we went our own ways

Alan had a great influence on my life; amongst other things he introduced me to Harold Craxton with whom I collaborated on several arrangements. Later on, Harold was also instrumental in getting me elected as an examiner for the Associated Board of the Royal Schools of Music. To digress for a moment: I was examining in Glasgow for the Board and a little lassie came in for a Grade II piano exam. After the preliminary salutations I asked her to play the scale of D major with the left hand only. There was no response. I asked again; still silence. At this I rose and approached the piano, asking if all was well; "Yes, she was fine", so again I asked her to play the scale of D major with the left hand only. At this, she burst forth in an agonised voice - "Please sir, which *is* my left hand?" From this engagement and from the many years I subsequently worked for the Board, I was able, from the fees they paid me, to lay down a goodly selection of vintage wine and port—some of which I still have to this day!

Harold Craxton was an inspiring teacher, musically interesting though somewhat weaker on the technical side. He had some renowned pupils, including Denis Matthews. We have a tendency to remember Harold as a great teacher but let us not forget that in earlier days he was a most eminent and sympathetic accompanist. It is good to see many of his recordings being reissued on CD.

But to return to Alan, he had a great feeling for Scotland; we often conversed in the vernacular for it was, after all, his native country, as it was mine. He longed to get back to his homeland but sadly failed to get a suitable appointment, though he and his second wife, Janet Craxton the distinguished oboe player, did eventually own a cottage in Mid Lothian. I, too, had a great longing to be in Scotland once again, so that it was a great joy to me when I was appointed Head of Music, BBC Scotland when I left the Aeolian Quartet. Alan was a very gifted composer of miniatures, and, as I am happy to say and much appreciate, wrote some very fine pieces for me.

While I was a student at the RAM I made music with

some other students who maintained friendship and collaboration with me for many years. David Carl Taylor was the leader of our string quartet while we were students. At that time we had ambitions to keep the ensemble going after we had left the Academy and entered professional life. Fate decreed otherwise but, as I recount elsewhere, we both became members of the Stratton Quartet and remained together until the war.

In the mid 1930s Myers Foggin and I teamed up as a viola and piano partnership and we remained together until the war. We recorded together on several occasions and the duo ensemble had great potential. He tried hard, as a recreation, to revive my flagging interest in golf, but to little avail. On one last fatal occasion, when I was playing particularly badly, we struggled on towards the final green. There was a pond away towards the left and I solemnly vowed that if my ball went anywhere near the water I would finally abandon this frustrating game. There was no need to go near the pond, but with the poor show I was making anything could happen—and did. I hit the ball fair, but not square, and off it went, flying like a homing bird right into the middle of the pond! I never wielded a club again from that day forth!

Frederick Grinke was to become a life-long friend and we remained in touch until his death in 1987. Both he and his close friend, the late David Martin, had come over from Canada on scholarships and decided, eventually, to stay on in England. Fred and I recorded together, played in the Boyd Neel Orchestra, joined the RAF together, and after the war we both became professors at the Academy. It was during a particularly dreary period of the war that talking together one day we commiserated with one another, 'We're not the kind of players to whom someone would lend a Stradivarius; we are not the kind of chaps to discover an important long lost manuscript in some old junk shop; nor are we the kind of lucky fellows to whom someone would leave a fortune'. Well, as luck would have it, I was lent the Archinto Stradivarius viola by the Royal Academy of Music shortly after the war. Then I had the good fortune in 1954 to find a long lost manuscript of a viola sonata by Alan Rawsthorne. When I first met Alan after the war I asked him if he had written anything for the viola, and as he answered in the negative I asked him if he would write something for me. Well, he had so many commitments at that time that, sadly for me, he refused the invitation. Imagine my surprise, therefore, when browsing in a second-hand music shop in Hampstead I came across a score of a viola sonata by Alan Rawsthorne! I immediately went to see him and challenged him, and when he still denied writing anything for viola I sang him the opening of the sonata which was no mean achievement! When he heard it, and of my extraordinary discovery, his eyes lit up and he enquired in astonishment as to how on earth I had found it. I explained the circumstances and he confessed to writing it immediately before the war. After the first performance he had sent it together with other of his manuscripts, to the West Country for safe keeping. Unfortunately there was an air-raid and the house where he had stored his precious scores received a direct hit, destroying all his valuable manuscripts. It transpired eventually that after the first performance of the viola sonata he had handed the piano score to a critic who was to write a detailed report on the work for the *Musical Times*. Came the war and the precious score was stored away in the critic's library to await better days. It was only the viola part which Alan Rawsthorne had sent away. So, all we had to do was to meet at the Hampstead dealer's establishment and settle the purchase. The dealer was pleased to see me, since the British Museum had now declared an interest in the score. I introduced him to the composer and he had the good grace to apologise for placing such a modest price on the manuscript—I think it was £4 or £5—and so, as Alan later recounted here he was with a Jew (the dealer) on one side, and a Scotsman (myself) on the other, insisting that, though the score was obviously his property he must pay a fiver in order to retrieve his work!

I later edited the work, with minor alterations, chiefly to the last movement, and it was published by O.U.P.

Now, as I later explained to Grinke, two of the wishes had been fulfilled. I had still to receive a fortune... I am still waiting!

Grinke and I used to meet periodically to discuss our respective students; I relieved him of some of his less promising ones, telling them that if they changed to the viola they would never be out of a job, a forecast which proved to be true. I remember Fred coming to me one day in despair over one dud student—even I refused to take him on as a viola pupil—but, as I explained to Fred, 'be kind to him, for who knows he may one day become a critic'! The student dutifully fulfilled my prediction, and gave his former professor a glowing notice! Such is fate!

Oddly enough my chief difficulty in making friends was not my shy approach, or possibly dour manner, but my sense of humour which was so different from that of the English. Mine was very basic—someone called it home-made! Their's was more sophisticated and subtle. I had difficulty in seeing the point. My harmony teacher used to tell me funny stories and at the appropriate moment I would laugh immoderately—but the point of the story usually eluded me. I suppose the national characteristics were so very different that my rather naive approach was out of gear. It took me some time to adapt myself to English ways, but once I had become acclimatised I felt very much at home, despite occasional difficulties. I little dreamed that I should spend the next forty years in London.

*The dearly beloved Queen's Hall had opened in 1883, presumably named after the then reigning monarch, Queen Victoria. Seating 2,500 people, it was closely associated with symphony concerts (I had expected and hoped to spend most of my musical life there), especially the Sir Henry Wood Promenade concerts which began to be held there annually from 1894, continuing every summer until this, the best of London's concert halls, was destroyed by a direct hit from one of Hitler's doodlebugs in 1941. It was never replaced. Such a peculiarly beautiful hall for music of all kinds whether recital, chamber music or orchestral. The acoustics were splendid—the Festival Hall was a disaster in comparison—and decorated a particularly soft green with gentle lighting. The only lack was bar facilities!

Chapter 3

Thoughts on Art?

When during studentship there was a blank Saturday morning, a stroll down to the Wallace Collection to view the pictures was my morning's entertainment; also to listen to the lectures on art. Rembrandt, Rubens, Gainsborough, Hoek, Velasquez, Murillo: all were there for my delectation, to be dissected, their variety of techniques examined, in fact a richly rewarding morning drinking in the beauty of art. Some, which in my innocence I admired, were dismissed by the lecturer as being meritorious but trivial; such as Boucher, Meissonier, Grevy and others of the French school, though no doubt they served their patrons well in their day. The collections of furniture and armour had little appeal for me, though maybe they made an impression.

Returning recently, hoping to revive old memories and savour the delights of bygone times, I found to my disappointment that the glories of my youth had lost much of their appeal, 'a thing of beauty' was not always a joy forever! 'Gather ye rosebuds while ye may' and learn to appreciate the joys of the moment, for they may not last forever.

It was the same with the Russian Ballet. While still playing at Covent Garden, the annual visit of the *Ballet Russe de Monte Carlo* invaded these shores every summer during the 'thirties. I was completely overwhelmed; no balletomane was ever more enthusiastic than me. Every dress, every movement, every bit of scenery and inflection of the story were treasured as revelations of beauty. It was, sadly, an infatuation that was doomed to die when in later years, on renewing acquaintance with the ballet, I found myself listening to the orchestra instead of watching what was happening on the stage. The once much admired movements struck me often as stale and unprofitable, gymnastic gestures, devoid of meaning or beauty.

However, Spanish dancing and the freedom of Greek music and movement are most exciting to me. I still recollect the joy my second wife Jean and I had in beholding three chaps, late one moonlit night beside the sea, spontaneously dancing the Zorba dance after dinner; it was entrancing.

Poetry is enjoyable, though in limited quantity. However, it is easier to assimilate and enjoy when read aloud. Shakespeare is paramount. Perhaps one can get a surfeit of over–indulgence in the arts, too much, too concentrated, in too little time. What vision the writer of Ecclesiastes displayed when he wrote, 'Vanity of vanities, all is vanity'. 'All things are full of weariness; the eye is not satisfied with seeing, nor the ear filled with hearing...' 'There is no new thing under the sun.' And herein lies the clue to the problem. It has been difficult to move into the 20th century, and appreciate the new developments in art; I have been content to be a traditionalist, favouring classical and romantic art. Well, perhaps there is still time, even though time is running out!

Many people dislike modern art, but what is modern art? Modern inventions, such as photography, recording, radio and television, and expert reproductions of various kinds, have knocked the old ideas sideways, so that the art of the great masters has become familiar, almost over familiar, to most interested people. But nothing in this world stands still, and artists, in whatever medium they work, have met—are meeting—the challenge, sometimes by new invention and sometimes by using the very inventions they have had to combat. In music, tonality has been swept overboard; dissonance has become acceptable; computers are able to imitate musical instruments and even invent new sounds. Rhythm has become more complex than anyone imagined possible. And this is modern music. I must confess to being tardy in accepting this new form of music making, perhaps because during my years in the Aeolian Quartet, traditional music was at its height and modern music frowned upon by everyone except the adventurous few. I still revere the traditional music, feeling sure it has not played itself out. Being a performer I am a poor listener, and listening to the great masters is carefully spaced out so as not to be heard too frequently, not so frequently as to become stale. In later years I have tended to explore works by the great composers which are not so familiar to me, e.g. the piano sonatas of Beethoven, the songs of Schubert, the operas of Mozart, and so on. There is a wealth of music here for me still to discover and enjoy, and this ties one to the great composers of the past. Vanity of vanities, all is not vexatious of spirit, though I did once find that yet another performance of the Brahms' violin concerto was more than I could abide!

Though museum art and organised concerts have lost much of their appeal, art in many of its aspects still has a profound effect on my life. My stepson, Michael, writes poetry which is deeply affecting. Our walls display pictures by living artists—many of whom our friends or acquaintances—and these have meaning and appeal in a very special way and are, in fact, a very necessary ingredient in our daily life, without which existence would lose much of its meaning. Music, of course, is the most important, especially what we play for ourselves; Jean and I managed until recently to play something by J.S.Bach every day, mostly my transcriptions of the violin and cello sonatas. These for our own delectation, playing them on the viola and not troubling overmuch about the sanctity of the composer's intentions. Art is there, after all, for one's enjoyment.

The poverty of the viola repertoire acts as a spur. We know what we like and pursue this idiom with ardour— and why not? Why, at our advanced ages, try to keep up with ideas which are uncongenial when there is still a wealth of classical music which is rarely played?

There does not appear to be so much suspicion towards modern music as was manifest during my active time of life, when to put a modern work in a programme was to arouse antipathy and empty the hall. Even when I was at the Royal Academy as Professor of Chamber Music, there was a blockage as regards modern music, and it was the same when, as Head of Music, BBC Scotland, I found the greatest difficulty in introducing anything new or experimental. Fortunately for our composers there has been a change of attitude in the public response and nowadays these things are healthier.

To create a work of art is a complex business, in that so many people eventually have to become involved. Obviously, the principal mover is the creator himself (or herself); his is, and remains, the sole inspiration during the work of creation. It is his experience of life, his imagination, his mind, his craftsmanship which is inviolate. He has to imagine the work through all its stages up to the finished form and he relies on his experience and craftsmanship, etc., to see it through. After this it is rare, however, that he can work in complete isolation. The play has to be acted, the book has to be read, the music listened to . . .there arises a kind of relationship of which he must, from time to time, become aware. Who or what sparks off the idea in the first place? Who sponsors the venture? All art is a form of communication, but communication with whom? And what kind of art is he involved in—commercial or fine art?

The creator chooses his medium; he works most frequently on his own, not in an ivory tower, but nevertheless with the idea that it must be communicable to other human beings. At its simplest the artistic creation makes a direct appeal. For instance, you paint or draw a picture and that's that; nothing and no one comes between you and your viewers. It is, in many ways, one of the simplest and most direct forms of communication. You write a poem, a short story, a novel and straightway you are surrounded by critics who are full of advice as to what you should have done. Even so, you are in direct communication with your readers.

But once you have to rely on someone else to present your creation you are in a much more complex situation. Few people read plays, and here you have to rely on a producer and actors to place your work before the public. Fewer people still can read a musical score and only a very small minority can hear, in the mind's ear, the probable result of the reading—and there is no means of finding out what kind of a mess the reader may be making of the music.

The composer of music puts down on paper directions for a performer to bring into sound, yet he has to rely on the performer to interpret his directions faithfully and at the same time hope that this player will present the music in an attractive performance. How closely does the performer realise the ideal of the composer? The obvious solution would seem to be for the composer to perform his own work; few composers, however, have either the time or energy or aptitude to become really good performers, though there are notable exceptions. Even so, suppose this ideal were to be realised, is each performance the same? As of course they do differ, which is the ideal performance? Is there a dichotomy between the artist as creator and the artist as performer? Do the composer and the performer present two different sides of the same coin? Is the whole affair a relationship—a very complex and frequently changing one—between the two music makers?

As a performer I have always been conscious of the debt I owe the composer—to some more than others. For instance, there is the debt I owe to composers of the past; not an easy debt to pay since conditions have changed over the years and even the instruments we play sound very different to those used in the composer's lifetime. But the composer's notes don't change, nor do his directions. How much freedom can the performer bring to his interpretation without unduly distorting the composer's ideas? In our time we have witnessed a return to instruments and bows as they were in olden times, and an attempt at realisations of style and ornamentation such as the composer might have approved. This fashion, while interesting historically, has not met with universal approval; but it seems to be one that has come to stay.

I compare this state of affairs to the problem of parents and children. One spends years training and bringing children up to be good citizens; then they go off to live independent lives and one is no longer responsible for their activities. So, too, when the composer has finished his task of creation, the pieces of music go off to live independent lives—no longer controlled by the parent hand. Life in the form of performers has taken over. All that the child has to go on is years of training in good habits; all that the music has to offer the player is a collection of black dots on a page, plus a lot of human feelings.

Chapter 4

Entering the Music Profession

Life was unfolding very pleasantly. It has given me luck and has continued to do so. During the years of my tuition, it was good simply to be playing, and obviously making decent progress. Composition was not, however of any great interest to me, and I displayed only a limited talent for it. But I did feel a keen interest in arranging music for my instrument, and the poor classical repertoire for the viola certainly fostered this. One of my most pleasant recollections of the various recitals I attended during this period, was of a programme in which all the works happened to be arrangements.

In retrospect I have only two regrets: one is that I did not become a singer, and the other that I scorned the academic life and missed the experience of a university career. I am therefore, delighted that my two sons, Sebastian and Rupert Oliver have realised these ambitions for me. Both went to Cambridge, Sebastian to King's and Rupert Oliver to St John's. Sebastian is a composer, and at the present time Professor of Music at the University of Surrey, while Rupert became a singer and was engaged first for some years in the Opera in Zurich, and later in Basel and now lives and works in Scotland. They have more than made up for any deprivation I may have felt.

Their mother, my first wife, Mary Hunt, had also been trained at the RAM as a pianist. I always hoped that together we would make a duo team, but it was not to be since she had too retiring a nature to be a performer. We had first met in my home town of St Andrews, she attending a summer school and I at home on holiday. The summer school was devoted to chamber music with the Menges Quartet as the resident performers, and with Harold Craxton and Herbert

Wiseman also in attendance. The evening concerts given by the Quartet were a feature of the course and were open to the public; these I attended. Ivor James, the quartet's cellist, introduced each work, discoursing on the composer and analysing the work with illustrations played by the quartet. This was an idea I was to adopt in late years and one which I found useful for bridging any barrier between the platform and the audience. Harold Craxton (who taught Mary) also introduced his pieces in a similar manner. Both Harold and Ivor were natural humorists, which greatly added to the enjoyment of these evenings. I recall a splendid performance of the B flat quartet by Brahms which features the viola, and how magnificently John Yewe Dyer played that evening; it was viola playing *par excellence.*

During the next few months Mary Hunt and I met many times and finally decided to get married. I was then twenty–seven, and quite ready to settle down to a more stable existence.

Getting a foothold in the profession was no easy business. Fortunately for me, the practice of putting a deputy in one's place when a better job materialised was quite rife. It was a practice of which I heartily disapproved but which I enjoyed to my advantage. There was once a visiting conductor who objected very strongly to the abuse of his several rehearsals by this habit, but he did notice that the horn player was present at all his rehearsals. At the final rehearsal on the day of the concert, he made a speech praising that player's devotion to duty, only to find that the chap he had so highly lauded would not be playing at the concert!

So I too was prepared to deputise, and consequently found myself on several occasions on my way to the theatre in Hammersmith to play in the pit for Sir John Martin Harvey in 'The Only Way'. It gradually got around that I was available, and I found myself in fairly steady demand in the theatres of Central London. Increasingly I was engaged for theatre orchestras on my own behalf, and played at the Vaudeville for the 'Co-Optimists', deputising for Philip Burton, the viola player of the Griller Quartet; at the Haymarket for several shows, and Her Majesty's at other times; I also played in the orchestra for Tauber in 'The Land of Smiles', and for the opening of The Cambridge Theatre. In this show, 'Charlot's Revue' with Beatrice Lillie and Anton

Dolin and that most charming actor J. H. Roberts, a young girl, Jean Beckwith, came down into the orchestra pit to sing a song. I remember being impressed by her distinguished manner. Little did I realise then that twenty five years hence I was to become her husband! She also appeared *in 'The Land of Smiles'* while I played in the pit—but a lot was to happen to both of us before we met after the war.

In those days, that is the early 1930s, I was ready to play for anyone in any capacity. I even auditioned for a jazz band, but turned it down because l didn't think the money was good enough! I always regret that I never played for silent films, since I am sure it would have been an experience to remember. However, the theatre kept me alert, and I soon became adept in keeping my place through a multitude of indifferent manuscript parts.

Sir Thomas Beecham formed his London Philharmonic Orchestra in 1932, and I had the good fortune to occupy a modest seat in the viola section. Let me say right away, this was a great experience. We had preliminary section rehearsals, for the wind, brass and strings on their own. At that time I only knew of Sir Thomas by repute and this merely conveyed a hazy idea of his prowess, his quixotic wit and his daring experiments. I had played under Sir Henry Wood at the RAM and consequently had learned a lot about orchestral discipline, as well as something of the orchestral repertoire, from that amazing man—a great inspiration. I was therefore all keyed up to do my best for Sir Thomas. My immediate reaction was one of disappointment; we bashed through a couple of pieces with Sir Thomas wagging his stick in an uninterested manner. Then we tackled a Mozart symphony; the same slap-dash attitude prevailed until the second subject. Suddenly he became electric, moulding the phrases with such sensitivity and intense musical perception that I found tears streaming down my face. I was enchanted, and ashamed; I was completely won over. From that time on, Sir Thomas could do no wrong. His Mozart was an endless joy. He would spend a considerable time over the nuance and phrasing of a melody. He had a carefully chosen team of players to carry out his wishes. Paul Beard led the orchestra with great efficiency and the other string principals were George Stratton, Frank Howard, Anthony Pini and Victor Watson.

All the Stratton Quartet, of whom I was a member, were in the orchestra and we had some fine players in the woodwind section including Leon Goossens and Reginald Kell.

On our first tour we had the great soprano Eva Turner who had such a big voice of true magnificence and it seemed to flower during the tour becoming more dominant and beautiful night after night. A towering personality! An unforgettable experience. Kreisler gave of his beauty of sound—and how seductive it was. Heifetz, too, bowled us over with his never failing technique and ardour. Apart from concerts, we also recorded with these artists. When Kreisler was recording the Mendelssohn concerto he had some trouble over the broken octaves near the beginning of the first movement. These were the early days of recording, (78 rpm records, four minutes a side and no chance to re-take or over-dub a mistake), how we all sympathised as he tried time after time to get it right and as eventually he succeeded we all cheered and he gave us one of his bewitching smiles. I recall also, when we recorded Beethoven's 5th with Koussevitzky, with whom we were enjoying a very sticky relationship, how he made the wrong four minute cut, and how we cheered at his mistake! I remember a recording session with Heifetz and how I was placed right beside him, an object lesson in fiddling if ever there was one. The recording engineer came out and said would Mr Heifetz care to make a test right away? Yes, he would, despite the early hour of 10.00 a.m. I was sorely disappointed! Heifetz laid into the violin with all the energy he possessed, producing the roughest tone imaginable. 'I'll play it back to you' said the recording chap, and I thought 'whatever will he think?' Well back it came with the most heavenly sound I'd ever heard! I had had my lesson, I went home and did some quick thinking about tone production.

These two violinists were indubitably the best but we also enjoyed the elegance and musicianship of Szigeti, we argued about Hubermann, praising his profound musicianship while criticising his tone quality. Carl Flesch was too academic. Beecham at one concert set too fast a tempo for Flesch, and kept to it despite the fact that he knew Flesch was struggling. He took a devilish delight in this kind of contretemps. There were many other soloists that frankly I don't remember all that vividly, but I do recall our very own Albert Sammons. Such a nice man! A brilliant violinist, and so very modest about his performances. He was particularly good in unaccompanied Bach, and I trace my devotion to the Solo Sonatas and Partitas entirely to his influence. My chief recollection of Casals on the platform was his insistence on playing a rather dull work by Tovey. Fournier we enjoyed very much, a most polished player with such a clean technique. We also had a gloriously flamboyant performance from Suggia—we enjoyed that—she also had the grace to listen to the second half of the programme from the auditorium!

Lionel Tertis was closely associated with the orchestra both as performer and, for a short time, as editor. He had the good idea that if he fingered and bowed all the string parts the same way, the results would be ideal, but it didn't work out and the idea lapsed. His pioneering zeal for the viola brought him in front of the orchestra with a meagre viola repertoire. I recall his performances in the Mozart *Concertante*, the *Suite* of Vaughan Williams, and a curious collection of short pieces, some very attractive and others just so-so.

William Primrose contributed an electrifying performance of the Walton Concerto which had us fairly gossiping about technique. His tempo was fast and exhilarating, which brought out the jazz elements most favourably. Many years later, when I was Head of Music at the BBC in Glasgow, I was given the great pleasure of entertaining William. I remember most vividly his surprise and delight when we showed him into his suite in the hotel which was filled with flowers. A great warmth of welcome for this outstanding artist and former 'Glasgow boy'.

Our other attractions as soloists were the pianists. Solomon, an outstanding artist with remarkable concentration and sensitivity, quite overwhelmed us with his performances which radiated a most happy personality. This was Solomon at his best, some time before his tragic breakdown in health. He had a keen dedication to the music. We had an equally happy, though quite different, relationship with Myra Hess, also a most sensitive pianist who, at this time, was just emerging as a real force in music-making, giving all the promise of the great performances that lay before her. Benno Moiseivitch produced a lovely tone from the piano, backed up by a formidable technique. There was an unique personality in all he undertook—also, something not always present in these exceptional players, a sense of humour. Our relationship with Artur Schnabel was not always so happy; he demanded absolute silence when he was rehearsing, a thing impossible to achieve when parts had to be marked and bowing discussed between leaders of the various sections. We found his playing of great stature, severe, inclining towards the academic, but monumental. If only we could have loved it more!

Rachmaninov playing his own works was a revelation. At a morning rehearsal he approached the piano as though he loathed it, and everyone connected with it! His very first arpeggio dispelled the gloom, and we were sitting on the edge of our chairs determined not to miss a note of his performance. If he was good at rehearsal, he was even better at the evening concert. His compositions sounded better in his own performances than they ever did when played by other pianists although Moiseivitch came nearest the ideal.

At the end of the concert season in London we played for a season of opera at Covent Garden, and for the Ballet Russe de Monte Carlo. The opera was dreadfully hard work, the ballet a much more relaxed affair. Beecham was at his best and his worst in the opera house! Impatient with singers and producers, his temper flared. Yet there were moments of rare delight—and humour. When the horse came on stage, in rehearsal, and proceeded in the course of nature to relieve itself, Beecham remarked "Ah, critic as well as performer"! On another occasion he asked a member of the orchestra his name, "Ball sir", "What?", "Ball, sir," "How singular". There are endless stories illustrating his quick wit and his devilish disregard for people's feelings, as when he pushed his walking stick through the window of the newly decorated Brighton Pavilion in order to get more ventilation in his dressing room.

I recall the sparkling performance by Supervia in Rossini's opera *La Cenerentola*—she died shortly afterwards giving birth to her baby. This was a tragic loss; a voice of such superb quality with a tremendous range—most effective in the lower notes. We did several performances of *Der Ring des Nibelung* by Wagner, in which I remember

Frieda Leider, and especially the robust voice of Melchior. But my memory is a little vague as I was placed with too little room to draw a full bow, right in front of the timpani, which has quite a degree of activity in *The Ring*! *Die Meistersinger* was a real slog for the viola section, since after the overture the violas have ten bars rest and spend the next four hours hard at it! It was memorable for me since my partner disgraced himself with the kind of gesture one would have loved to have indulged in oneself, if only one had had the nerve! It was during the catch-as-catch-can scene of Beckmesser, and the singer was fairly messing around with his part. Suddenly my partner said, 'Oh, to Hell' and played a fortissimo chord of C major right across the strings of the viola. Consternation! One could almost see the chord floating across the auditorium and winging its way up to the Gods! I forget whether he got a round of applause.

Tristan und Isolde under Beecham was a revelation of sensuous delight although not everyone was equally affected. I heard one player remark at the end of the performance, 'I think I'll go to bed with an aspirin'. *Der Rosenkavalier* was a mad frolic with such outrageous rubato—it's the only time I enjoyed Strauss in the opera house. Usually I found him a longwinded bore, with too few moments of music to admire. Then we had *Schwanda the Bagpiper* by Weinberger with its lilting tunes, so immediately engaging. Every violinist at the time loved to play the *Polka* as a solo. We had several tenors from Italy singing *bel canto* and trying to out-flank Caruso in power—none of them memorable. I got hopelessly lost in the first pages of Puccini's *La Boheme*—it goes so fast I seemed to be turning pages all the time—too late! How I loved that opera, even so.

The Ballet Companies brought their own conductors with them. We played the standard ballets including *Les Sylphides*, *Swan Lake* and *Petrushka*. The London audiences went mad about the ballet, and 'House Full' notices were the order of the day. Books were written about the company and the chief dancers; Danilova Riabouchinska, Massine and others were lionised and became household names. I must confess that I enjoyed what I could see from the orchestra pit. It was all so fresh and new and full of verve and life. The season took place in the summer months and the orchestra suffered from the excessive heat and especially during matinees the awful stench which came up through the floor boards of the orchestral pit—a century of rotting cabbages, or so we thought. At that time and for a considerable period before, the fruit and vegetable market of Covent Garden was just around the corner. However, all things considered, the orchestra maintained a reasonable standard and some of the solos were brilliantly played.

What happened on the stage dictated the tempo of the music. Some of the phrasing in consequence was exceedingly square—but we had our moments of glory. One evening both conductors were unwell and they eventually got Sir Thomas Beecham to deputise. The music was the *Polovtsian Dances* from *Prince Igor* by Borodin. Now we had given brilliant performances of this music on the concert platform with Beecham, and that evening's performance was no exception. Constant messages were passed down from the stage, 'Slower, Sir Thomas, slower', but Beecham took no notice and concentrated on the brilliance of his performance. Finally the end came, with the dancers in a muddled heap on the stage. 'That made the buggers hop' was Sir Thomas's only comment! Massine in *The Three Cornered Hat* was really superb. He was the only male dancer I have known who could wear that impossible garb and remain truly manly in bearing. There was no fraternisation between members of the orchestra and the Ballet Company; they conformed to a very strict discipline which they seemed to enjoy, though it must have been very burdensome on occasions. We, the orchestra, behaved in a mildly rebellious manner, fretting as we did over the repeated routine performances, all except the cellists who had their backs to the stage but managed to fix up a large mirror to the top of their music stands and were thus happily entertained.

The orchestra gave concerts during the winter months as well as touring and recording. The concerts given by Beecham included those for the Royal Philharmonic Society, and the Courtauld-Sargent concerts were conducted by the dapper Malcolm Sargent. These two conductors gave us a completely different approach to rehearsal, Sir Thomas being easy going for the first play–through of the work in hand (and even the second play through), realising that the players themselves would correct obvious faults in reading, so only then getting down to the finer details of performance. In contrast, Sargent would give us a wonderful display of virtuosity with the stick but somehow failed to get his desired results from the orchestra. Every work was rehearsed in small sections, which would be analysed and commented upon—even sung sometimes! We rarely played through a movement to get to know the musical idea of the composer. At the evening concert I would look at the pages of the viola part and often wonder if we had actually played the piece! The results were not ideal; even solos were remodelled after Sargent's desire. It hardly sounded like the same orchestra that Sir Thomas had galvanised into life. Sargent was at his best with choirs, whose members adored him—orchestral players were diffident about him—such a strange mixture.

Since both Sir Thomas and Sir Malcolm had charge of the same orchestra, the London Philharmonic, there was a certain amount of rivalry between them, sometimes friendly but not always so. Sir Thomas, with his well known caustic tongue always referred to his colleague as 'Flash Harry'. Once when Sargent was unwell Beecham was heard to remark, "Nothing trivial, I hope", and again when Sir Malcolm was recounting his travels abroad with the orchestra, and mentioned he had been fired upon by the Arabs, Sir Thomas' comment was, "Oh, I had no idea the Arabs were so musical!".

We had several guest conductors: I remember Felix Weingartner with his Viennese charm, also Bruno Walter with his meticulous regard for expression marks. Our pianissimo could never be soft enough for him even when we just placed the bow on the string and made no sound he would still protest that it was too loud! Both conductors contributed admirable performances in their individual ways.

But time and events marched on. George Stratton was asked to be leader of the London Symphony Orchestra, and getting leave of absence became more difficult. Gradually during the next year or two we all left the Philharmonic and joined the London Symphony Orchestra. I stayed with this orchestra until the end of the war, eventually becoming joint leader of the viola section. While I had been with

Beecham I had enjoyed the supreme brilliance of the orchestra at its best. I often thought that maybe, one day, I would take part in performances which, in a different way, would give me complete satisfaction but I knew that never, though I lived to be a hundred, would I take part in better or more exciting performances than those conducted by Sir Thomas. As it transpired, I never did. My work with the London Philharmonic Orchestra was to remain the high water mark of my orchestral experience and I will always be grateful for it.

Surprisingly, not everyone was enthralled. I remember having a ride in the tube train after a particularly splendid performance. My neighbour was a double bass player. I mentioned how much I had enjoyed the performance and he seemed surprised. 'Didn't you like the Beethoven?' 'No.' 'You must have enjoyed the Rossini.' 'No.' 'Didn't you enjoy anything?' 'No, you see, I don't like music.'! I have always regarded double bass players since then with a degree of scepticism!

At about this time I joined the Boyd Neel Orchestra—a string orchestra of about twenty players, led by 'Punch' Willoughby, and later on by Frederick Grinke. This was a very democratic organisation. Very unruly: everyone had a right to have his say about the interpretation at rehearsal— "it was too loud", "no, too soft", or, "it was too fast", "no, too slow", and so on. Meanwhile the conductor, Boyd Neel, waited until we had a quorum of opinion and proceeded to conduct accordingly. Bearing in mind the chaos at rehearsal, we gave, to everyone's surprise, some very fine performances sparkling with life. Boyd Neel had a very clear beat and was sensitive enough to follow the orchestra from time to time. Yet he had authority when required. Our concerts were great—but tiring, and how I missed the timpani at climaxes! Our recordings were superb and set a new standard of performance at that time. Most of the players were young—some just beyond student age—and this added zest to all we played. After the war the orchestra somehow lost its momentum and eventually Boyd Neel took up an administrative post in Canada.

Chapter 5

Quartet Playing

While keeping a wary eye on the financial aspects of my activities I was in no way neglecting the more serious side of the profession. The quartet we had established as students at the Royal Academy of Music broke up as we dispersed at the end of our tuition. We had enjoyed considerable success, being spurred on by the enthusiasm of our professor, Bertie Withers—no great teacher but an inspiring one who cultivated in us a love of string quartets which I maintain to this day. I was also helped by my two professors, Marjorie Hayward and Raymond Jeremy, both of whom had been associated with string quartets for many years.

But it was not to be as I had planned, and I was left floating around grasping any chance of quartet playing or ensemble work. When I played with the Schwiller Quartet we had some limited success at the South Place Sunday evening concerts, and performed many out of the way works as well as some of the classics. My association with the South Place concerts dates from 1932 so before I gave up quartet playing on leaving London at the end of 1963 I had performed there nearly a hundred times. We played for a miserable fee—a guinea each player—until, many years later as a member of the Music Committee of the Arts Council, I was instrumental in having the fee increased, not by as much as we had hoped for, but more in keeping with social events.

My former colleague, David Carl Taylor, had meantime joined the Stratton String Quartet—how I envied him his good fortune—a quartet which had a fair number of engagements and commanded a good following on the radio. It had been formed in 1927 but had suffered a few changes in personnel. The original viola player died of tuberculosis and his successor Frank Howard, principal viola with the LPO, died soon after from the same disease. Imagine my good fortune when, on David Taylor's recommendation, I was elected to the position. My elation was slightly dampened in the watches of the night by the thought that I, too, might meet an untimely death, but I manfully put the thought aside and plunged into the activity of establishing my new-found position.

1933 was a great year for me—it was my very first recording, no less than the Elgar String Quartet and Piano Quintet with Harriet Cohen. The leader of the quartet, George Stratton, had a few years previously played the Elgar Violin Concerto to the composer, who was mightily impressed. Elgar himself chose our quartet to make the first recordings of these two major works. As he wrote to Gaisberg of HMV, 'If you do the quintet I think Miss Harriet Cohen should do it, and the Stratton people have enough go and force which some of the other quartets do not possess'. We were highly honoured. In fact, Elgar asked to hear this recording when he was lying in bed during his last illness. True, these same works had not had a good reception from the critics, but we found them most rewarding. Harriet Cohen was not perhaps the ideal partner because she had small hands and found some of Elgar's writing for the piano rather hard to manage, but she was musical and gave a good account of the work. She had signed photos of Elgar, Sibelius, Bax and many prominent people from other walks of life on her piano, so as well as her professional engagements she must have led a pretty busy social life. The recordings went off easily, except that these were the days when each movement had to be carved up into four-minute episodes to suit the length of the record. We had hoped to put the slow movement of the quartet on to one side only and we gave what we felt was a very fine performance only to be told that it was a few seconds too long (I leave it to the reader to imagine our consternation and the language that this announcement caused!). However, in the end we decided to play the music a little faster—not without trepidation—but all went well with the second 'take' and we were mightily relieved when we got Elgar's approval.

I remember that our first broadcast consisted of a Haydn quartet and the Debussy quartet—no mean task for the changed ensemble, although we came through the ordeal with flying colours. I was also faced with six concerts during the season at Bexhill-on-Sea at which we had to perform Haydn quartets, three or four at each concert. They were all new to me. I was astonished at the enthusiasm for these quartets displayed by both George Stratton and our distinguished cellist, John Moore, an enthusiasm I couldn't then honestly share. I think I was too engrossed in trying to remember the themes, and especially the tunes of the minuets, which tended to sound very much alike. After a few years of performing Haydn, however, I gradually became an admirer and finally had so much enthusiasm for the quartets as to place Haydn in the forefront of quartet composers. Later, I was approached by a publisher to compile an album of easy quartet movements by Haydn, a proposition I eagerly embraced. To my utter amazement, I then found that there are no easy quartet movements by Haydn! Each movement seems to have some passage work, usually for the first violin, which requires an advanced technique.

The Haydn and Beethoven quartets became my favourite repertoire, though for widely differing reasons; the Beethoven are majestic and awe-inspiring, the Haydn have a more homely atmosphere. One can love Haydn, but Beethoven has the ability to stir the soul, especially in his later quartets. We carried a large and ever changing repertoire which we played for music clubs, universities and for such famous concerts as those at South Place, where on 6th October 1935 our recital was the first to be broadcast from Conway Hall.

My colleague John Moore is a very loveable man with a most attractive personality and is still, in his nineties, quite the most handsome man I have ever met. He is also a musician of rare distinction. Quite apart from music, he had enormous charisma, and for me, he was a God who could do no wrong, and I found myself modelling my actions on his way of life. Being at that age somewhat vain, I was always distressed when taking bows to the audience, that all the women were looking, not at me, but at John!

In the early days, when I was still a bit puritanical in my outlook, I recall our first Wigmore Hall recital. I arrived early in the artists' room to be joined presently by John who confessed that he had had a drink on the way in, to fortify his courage for the difficult cello solo at the beginning of the recital. I was horrified—drinking before such an important event! Furthermore, he was not sure whether he shouldn't have had another, just to be quite secure; whether I dissuaded him I am not sure. I thought he played magnificently—but he was disappointed and said, 'I knew I should have had that second drink'. (This was one habit that I never emulated.) He stayed with the quartet for twenty-eight years and I was indeed sorry when he announced his retirement.

George Stratton taught me most of the things I know about quartet playing, not so much by what he said, but by example. In the matter of quartet discipline and technique, I owe him much more than I realised at the time. He was a natural fiddler with an amazing inborn talent for discerning the musical structure of a composition and was highly regarded in the profession for his ability and integrity as a musician. We were indeed lucky to have him as a leader for the best part of fourteen years. He left to give all his time to his appointment as leader of the London Symphony Orchestra, in succession to Willie Read. He died just as he was beginning to make his name as a conductor, a sad loss to music.

My old colleague, David Carl Taylor, second violin in the quartet, was killed during the war—a tragic loss—and in 1944 we decided to re-name the quartet the Aeolian String Quartet

John Moore had looked after the business side of the quartet, and most admirably he dealt with it. When I took over this unenviable job in the early 1940s, I endeavoured to emulate his well established acumen. As managing director and under my aegis we always replaced the leaving member by a younger man. I hold no brief for a quartet retaining the same personnel year after year. The result is not good, as the lack of fresh ideas makes for staleness. It has always seemed enviable when a quartet stays together year after year, but it is a dangerous path to follow. A quartet never stays static in its achievements, and almost invariably the lack of fresh members results in stereotyped performances. Nor do I advocate that the members of a quartet should keep to quartet playing and never indulge in other musical activities. One can become too inbred, so the players should lead the life of active musicians with as much variety as possible.

We were a popular ensemble, young and enthusiastic, living a busy life travelling the length and breadth of the country and occasionally venturing abroad. In the spring of 1939 we visited Poland, sponsored by the British branch of the International Society for Contemporary Music, accompanied by Sir Arthur Bliss, playing his quartet and the second quartet by Elizabeth Lutyens. It was just at the time when Britain had guaranteed Polish independence and we were given a hero's welcome—alas, how we let them down—not by our playing, l hasten to add, but by our politicians.

Of all our travels, perhaps the most enjoyable was our tour of Austria. This happened directly after the war was over. We were due to stay in hotels commandeered by the British Forces, and to our delight were put up in the famous Sacher's Hotel, just beside the Opera House which had suffered badly from our bombing. We were issued with BAFS—Forces money—and found ourselves paying the equivalent of sixpence for an aperitif. Consequently we raided the Forces NAAFI and replenished our wartime dwindling reserves of clothes and toiletries. We were astonished at the contrasts between the occupying Forces. The Russians had a ring of machine-guns permanently manned around their hotel. The Americans had sentries with loaded guns outside, but the British hotel was unguarded— one could stroll in and out without let or hindrance! We had enough free time to visit one of Beethoven's houses. John Barbirolli, who was in Vienna at the same time and accompanied us on our expeditions, remarked on the narrow winding staircase leading to Beethoven's flat, saying, 'The old boy would have had to have kept reasonably sober to negotiate these stairs'. We also went to the room where Schubert died, a pathetically small room with only a bedstead. At the library attached to the Musikverein we were received by the charming old lady who was in charge. We asked if we could see an original manuscript, "Which one", asked our lady, "If possible the 9th Symphony in C Major", we replied, and in no time at all she produced it. We were fascinated by the emendations Schubert had made to the score, most meticulous and telling. We also saw a performance of *Aida*, given in the old Opera House where Beethoven was accommodated during his composition of *Fidelio*. But it was a sad city, only a shadow of its former glory. We gave two concerts in Vienna, one in Graz, and one in Klagenfurt. During our stay in Graz the Commanding Officer of the British Forces who had been detailed to look after us asked if we would give a concert for the children during the afternoon, which we were delighted to do. Among other things we played the Austrian Hymn with variations, which forms the slow movement of Haydn's String Quartet *'The Emperor'* Op. 76, No.3, which was quite new to the children! As we steamed out of Vienna on our way home, our leader took out his fiddle and started to play Kreisler's tune 'Old Vienna', which brought tears to our eyes.

Incidentally, while in Vienna we were introduced to a Miss Rasoumovsky—a direct descendant of the Count Rasoumovsky to whom Beethoven dedicated his Op. 59 string quartets.

We played at the first post-war International Festival in Prague, before the communists came to power, and also toured Northern Italy with great success, visiting, amongst other places, Cremona, the home of violin making. We went to the Stradivarius workshop and saw his tools and also the mould around which he fashioned the Archinto Viola—the very same instrument I had with me! What a thrill that gave me!

The quartet also played in Paris for the British Council, and broadcast before an invited audience who chatted to each other throughout the broadcast. It was not the happiest of performances!

We came home from all these trips abroad feeling we had accomplished much for British music (we always played a British composition in each programme) but financially at a loss. We did the pioneering work from which later ensembles were to reap the benefit (and increased fees). However, we enjoyed our concerts and it was fun being received by distinguished foreigners!

It was a trying time for British artists. With the end of the war musicians who had served in the Forces were returning to civilian life once more and were eager to re-establish themselves. On the other hand, music clubs—

and the BBC—who had had to make do with the mainly British musicians who had been around, had been starved of the vitalising element of foreign competition, and so it became a tough time for the home product. Sir Steuart Wilson, newly appointed Head of the Music Section of the Arts Council, came to the rescue of half a dozen quartets of which the Aeolian was one, by offering each a substantial sum to pay for extra rehearsals in order to re-establish the native talent. This was a godsend for us and, in retrospect, I think we made the most of it. The grant lasted for three years and certainly helped us to put our name once more before the public. It was perhaps unfortunate that the scheme worked in isolation from the British Federation of Music Societies and the BBC, since our chief difficulty remained— namely getting enough work to justify the grant we were receiving and which helped to keep us going. But, keep going we did, with increasing zeal and success as time went on.

And so we settled down, facing up to the perennial problems of quartet repertoire, and resolving them in new ways. We quickly became the most frequently broadcast quartet and therefore had to carry an enormous repertoire. We never refused an engagement and wandered through many undistinguished works as well as the standards of Haydn, Mozart, Beethoven, Schubert and Dvorak etc. Our programmes contained little Mozart since we felt that the composer was not at his best in these works. We delighted in the String Quintets, but reserved our chief praise for the Operas in which the truly great Mozart is appreciated.

The great music critic of post-war years, Ernest Newman, must have had similar feelings regarding Mozart when he wrote:

"Mozart is a myth, a legend, and the average musician no more thinks of revising the traditional notion of him, than a savage thinks of questioning the divinity of Mumbo-Jumbo. The orchestra seemed emptier than usual, and heaven knows how empty some of these instrumental works by Mozart can be. We were merely listening to the prattle of a bright child."

Anyone who has played the viola part of a Mozart Piano Concerto will surely agree.

But Ernest Newman, like many another critic, was not infallible. He once gave the Quartet a glowing notice for a

Bartok Quartet when we had, in fact, played Kodaly. Anyone can nod off on occasion! His championship of Wagner was an inspiration over which he could get carried away:

> "Next week," wrote Ernest Newman
> "It will be Schumann",
> But next week came, and it was Wagner,
> Just the same!

But we cannot leave Mozart in the lurch. No-one can be more irritating when off form but we must forgive him when we recall the sublime works he produced when the spirit moved him — as it often did.

Through many vicissitudes we managed, by temporary appointments, to keep going, though it was never very easy. Eventually, towards the end of the war we settled down with Alfred Cave and Leonard Dight as violins, and though not an ideal solution, this arrangement lasted for several years and established the Aeolian Quartet as a force to be reckoned with in English music. Eventually, to meet the challenge of a new crop of young and eager quartets, we had to look to our laurels and re-form with new players. We held auditions but to no avail, the orchestral scene and recording sessions were attracting all the good talent— where the money flowed, the good players flocked.

One day, as we were discussing how we could find a replacement leader for the quartet, the door bell rang and there before me was a young, thin, scrawny looking lad who said, 'I hear you are looking for a new leader for the Aeolian Quartet. Am I too late to apply?' "Step right in", was my reply. He explained that he was having lessons with Enesco in Paris, so could we postpone the audition until his return in a fortnight's time? We agreed, and fourteen days later the audition took place. He hadn't been playing for long before I looked at John Moore and we nodded in agreement. Behold! We had found in Sydney Humphreys our new leader. He was to stay with us for many years, only leaving shortly after I myself retired from the quartet. In no time at all he had stamped his personality on the quartet; he was a born leader in every way. His intonation was impeccable and his facility for grasping the essentials of a new work were quite outstanding. He had a formidable technique, as well as some idiosyncrasies which led to great arguments, but these were quickly resolved (and were probably quite healthy) and easily assimilated by the three of us. With Sydney we shot right ahead and quickly re-established our reputation as one of the leading British string quartets.

At the same time we were lucky to recruit Trevor Williams as second violin. He was a most gifted violinist who had a splendid flair for the fiddle and also played the piano rather well. I remember he played Paganini Caprices for his audition and astonished us with his commanding technique.

With our stalwart cellist, John Moore, we now had a team to challenge all rivals (including the influx from abroad) and were a formidable force. Sadly, in due course, John Moore retired from the quartet after twenty-eight years of devoted service. It was a great loss, and we were most fortunate in finding, as a replacement, Derek Simpson, a rising star and one of the most talented 'cellists it has ever been my luck to run across. Derek brought a new dimension to our activities and was a powerful influence on our future progress. He had the most beautiful tone quality which he could shape with an endless subtlety of nuance. He was influential in bringing our repertoire up to date with works by Bartok, Schoenberg, etc.

But it wasn't all hard slog—we did have our hilarious moments. On one occasion when we were playing at Blackheath Music Club, we arrived a little early as was our custom, to see that the lighting, music stands and chairs were to our satisfaction. That night I insisted that the rather decorative but unsuitable chairs should be replaced by a set of wooden kitchen chairs. This is important especially for the cellist. It was at the end of the first quartet as we rose to take the applause that the incident happened. I found to my chagrin that I couldn't dislodge myself from the chair. The joints at the back of the chair had come slightly apart and the tails of my coat had become wedged firmly in the gap, so while my colleagues bowed and left the platform I raised my posterior as far as I dared and acknowledged the clapping, waving my friends back to take more applause, meantime working frantically, but hopefully and secretly, to liberate myself from the chair—no easy task with a viola in one hand and a bow in the other. Finally, as my efforts were of no avail, I wrenched myself free accompanied by the sound of rending cloth, and finally made my exit holding on to a flapping tail!

On another occasion we had booked into a rather nice hotel and had noted that in the basement there was a very fine billiard table. During the intervals between quartets we reminded each other of the pleasant time we would have playing billiards after the concert. We hurried back and, fortunately, the room was free so we prepared to play. We were persuaded by our leader, who swore he knew the rules, that snooker was more fun than billiards and as none of us had had much experience of wielding a billiard cue, it was all one to us so we embarked on our game. Presently, as the bar closed, various guests strolled in and started to watch us playing and since we were still in evening dress we must have made an impressive spectacle. This however was short-lived; we missed ball after ball, we couldn't pot a single one. Restive sounds from our audience began to be very pointed. Just as things were reaching a climax of despair, the telephone rang and we said with one voice, 'That will be our call from Switzerland', and hastily beat an ignominious retreat, accompanied with sighs of relief from the long-suffering guests!

I have often been amazed at the erudition displayed by some amateur musicians who have had the time to explore the bye-ways of music and seem intent on putting us professionals on the rack, hoping no doubt to expose our ignorance! It can be most disconcerting. Fortunately these people are the exception, but they do keep us up to the mark. During my years in the Aeolian String Quartet we were constantly plagued by music lovers who knew all the Bartók quartets and this at a time when we only knew and played the second. They had records and scores and knew them intimately. The only solution seemed to be to organise a Bartók Series, and this we did in the 1959/60 season in our regular series in the Recital Room at the Royal Festival Hall. This turned out to be such a success that we had to repeat it several times throughout the British Isles. For a number of years we were invited by the late Dr Chalmers Burns, Director of Music at Newcastle University, to give a week's concerts on six successive evenings. One year we gave a Beethoven cycle and on another Mozart's ten celebrated quartets plus his string quintets and we also successfully repeated our Bartók series.

At the end of this marathon we felt able to meet our amateur enthusiasts on equal terms.

Chapter 6

The War Years and After

At the beginning of World War II in 1939, pacifism was not in the forefront of my mind. Like many others I did work in Air Defence, learning first aid and volunteering the car for the transport of casualties. At twenty-nine years old I was not immediately called upon to join the colours but nevertheless, the thought was constantly nagging away that somehow I should be more involved in the war effort.

It was in 1940 that my colleague, Frederick Grinke, telephoned with an idea that appealed to me. The Royal Air Force Music Department under its Director, Rudolph O'Donnell, was asking for musicians in groups of five to volunteer as complete units to tour the airfields and give concerts of light music to the troops, especially to the lads in France. I found the idea immediately attractive, particularly as our quintet was to contain the pianist Denis Matthews, Gerald Emms and Frederick Grinke, violins, and James Whitehead, a renowned 'cellist. It meant, in fact, that I would be playing music all the time, and one of my subconscious dreads had been the possible divorce from my viola that would arise when I was eventually called up. True, I would be volunteering a year or two before I was required to enlist, but the possibility of putting my viola playing to good use was not to be sneezed at. And so I found myself being fitted-out in Air Force blue at Uxbridge and square bashing my way through basic training at Bridgnorth.

It was, indeed, a change of life style! It took me some time to settle to the discipline of Air Force life and I confess that I never really liked it, and only submitted to it under duress. Some of it was necessary, I freely admit, but much of it was a waste of time and most frustrating. However, I got through these weeks somehow, and they were not without their lighter moments. Grinke, in an excess of zeal, had played at the camp concert one evening. At the line-up next morning our sergeant treated us to the usual crude comments on our appearance. He stopped in front of Grinke (who, misguidedly, at least expected some compliments on his performance) and uttered his only comment—'Are you the ****** who played the fiddle last night?'

I remember how one night we were sent out on guard duty and given a rifle with a specially blunted bayonet in case we hurt ourselves. Retrospectively I believe that was the only time I did guard duty during my five years of service with the RAF. Cleaning and polishing a worthless piece of linoleum was a daily chore in our barrack quarters. I remember paying a chap sixpence to do my stint while I found a room in which to practise the viola, and was he pleased to get it! The sergeant also laid on sarcasm with a heavy trowel—"Call me John—and when you get to know me better you'll learn to say, Yes, Sergeant!"

During our training, France fell. This put paid to all our plans of touring Air Force units in France to bring entertainment to the troops. We returned to Uxbridge (which was to become our headquarters for the rest of the war) to find ourselves in a goodly company of musicians—all those quintets who had volunteered to serve, now milling around with nothing to do. We spent a whole glorious summer getting lost in the long grass, sometimes rehearsing and building up a repertoire of light music, occasionally wondering what fate had in store for us.

Our life was not without its compensations. We were housed in a block of huts which had originally been built to accommodate prisoners of war during the First World War and which had subsequently been condemned as unfit for human habitation! The sudden influx of so many personnel was more than the authorities could cope with, and so we were encouraged—those who could—to live at home. This meant of course a daily trek to Uxbridge to report for duty at 8.00 am (later revised to 9.00 am) and a return journey each afternoon at 4.00 p.m. (later changed to 12.00 noon). Thus our life became bearable, even enjoyable in some respects, intermingled with stretches of boredom. Eventually we were grouped together to form an orchestra and, as such, we travelled to RAF stations in England, playing for the entertainment of the troops and also appearing on official occasions to lend glamour to the proceedings!

We rarely mixed with other RAF personnel, though we did have a rather severe, foul-mouthed Sergeant for a brief period. He tried, unsuccessfully, to instil into us some regard for a book containing the King's Regulations. Once, when we were on parade, one of our number arrived on a bicycle rather late and cycled up between the two ranks drawn up on parade. We expected the usual explosion from the sergeant, but no, we could almost see him flicking the pages of the King's Regulations trying to find a reference to 'misbehaviour on a bicycle'—alas there was nothing to discover. That was the end of our sergeant's liaison with us. One of our band arrived by taxi one morning and was saluted at the guard room and passed through as a VIP.

I was now dubbed Aircraft hand/musician, second-class (there was no third class as far as I could discover!). As such we were officially the lowest form of life in the RAF but at least we were still pursuing our profession, in which we counted ourselves very fortunate. Rudolph O'Donnell was not the world's finest conductor. He was adequate and keen, though unpredictable, but it was due to his perseverance that despite Ministry of War quibbles we continued to exist as an orchestra right through the war. For this we must pay our respects to him and, while very conscious that compared to the fighting forces our efforts were very puny, I think we did some good towards keeping up the spirits of the troops and, indeed, the general public.

But although we were classed as a non-combatant unit, we were very much aware of the war raging all around us. Because of shortage of accommodation, most of us lived out of camp, some in lodgings, but quite a number at home in London. Our nightly slumbers were disturbed by German air-raids and the sound of our anti-aircraft guns firing. Making our way to report daily at Uxbridge we were made very conscious of the horrendous amount of damage the people of London were standing up to with unabated courage and good humour, from the air raids, and later the doodle-bugs. Casualties were high. Not only that, we went every now and again to operational camps around Britain and brought our style of entertainment to the war-weary Air Force. We would see the aircraft taking off for the nightly raids over Germany, and the following morning experienced the anxiety of counting the number of planes that had returned safely. It was a harrowing experience. We played for memorial services, we played at the opening presentation of new war films, and we played for propaganda broadcasts for the BBC which were transmitted throughout the world.

Having a certain amount of free time, and having in our orchestra such players as David Martin, Harry Blech, Leonard Hirsch, Max Gilbert, Harvey Phillips, James Merritt, not to mention amongst the brass and woodwind players Dennis Brain, Leonard Brain, Gareth Morris, Edward Walker and Norman del Mar, also as pianists Howard Ferguson and Leonard Isaacs (I cannot recall all the names, especially since there were several periods when some players were seconded to other units), it is not surprising that we were in some demand for concerts and broadcasting. The BBC used us, and so did the National Gallery mid-day concerts, while occasionally we would be released for an important engagement elsewhere—but only in a strictly limited capacity. Ensembles important to the British concert world were thus kept functioning.

Once, Grinke and I were playing through Mozart's *Symphonie Concertante* when O'Donnell, who was conducting, was called away. We persuaded Harry Blech to try his hand with the baton. This was the first time he had conducted an orchestra, and he liked it so much he went on to establish himself as the very successful founder/conductor of the London Mozart Players.

We always appeared in uniform on the platform. If our Commanding Officer was in a good mood we would be let off in time to catch the 11.45 train from Uxbridge, which got us to the National Gallery in reasonable time for the 1 o'clock concert. If he was feeling mean, it would be the 12 o'clock train, which got us there just in time to rosin the bow, grab the music and mount the platform. On one occasion I arrived in time to have a word with Dame Myra Hess (whose idea it had been to instigate the daily concerts which were such a blessing to so many war-weary folk in London). She said she always played at a concert with full devotion as if it were her last appearance; that day I got on the platform and halfway through the first page of some unaccompanied Bach I thought, 'If I don't improve, this <u>will</u> be my last concert'! Another time, on arrival, I got there in the nick of time to perform with the quartet only to find everyone in disarray; an unexploded bomb had hit the gallery during the night and the disposal squad were still working on it. Presently word came through that all was well, the bomb had been defused and it was safe for the concert to proceed so we embarked on Beethoven's *Rasoumovsky* Quartet in F, Op 59 No.1 It was during the very tricky second movement—Beethoven's little game of using one note rhythmically repeated—that the explosion occurred. Consternation! Some people immediately rose to get out to safety, others cowered beneath their seats—we just played on. Personally I was counting the beats like blazes since it is an easy movement in which to get lost. Presently people began to realise that the explosion had taken place in another part of the gallery and that the gallant quartet were still intent on playing, so they began to applaud us! I think we were all relieved, players and audience, when we launched into the succeeding movement—Adagio Molto!

In my spare time at Uxbridge I scored the whole of Bach's *Art of Fugue*, copying out all the parts. Eventually we launched it at a National Gallery concert and at the South Place Sunday evening concerts. After a broadcast on 19th September 1944 I received the following letter from Sir Steuart Wilson:

> *Broadcasting House, London W1*
> *20th September 1944*
>
> *Dear Watson,*
> *I listened last night to 'Kunst der Fuge'. I am ashamed to say that I had not heard it before and had no idea that it was so beautiful and restful, and I think I never spent a more pleasant forty-five minutes with the score on my knees and peace in my heart, a good dinner to follow, and I owe you my sincere thanks for all the trouble you have taken in it.*
> *Yours, Steuart*

The Grinke-Forbes-Phillips String Trio, which had been active during the war, (Lennox Berkeley dedicated his String Trio to us in 1944), was no longer a viable unit once the war was over. We had profited by being together in the RAF which had made rehearsal easy, but back in 'civvy' street we each went our different ways. I re-formed the Trio with Maria Lidka (violin) and Vivian Joseph (cello) and we became the London String Trio. This was a useful ensemble which thrived well.

Maria Lidka was a very classical player, which was ideal for the Beethoven and Mozart trios. Even so, we performed many modern pieces. Elizabeth Maconchy's Trio was one of a number of works especially written for the ensemble and we gave the first European performance of Schoenberg's String Trio, an interesting but not a very likeable work. Vivian Joseph played with a big, warm, sensuous tone which always did full justice to a melody, such as he had in the slow movements of the trios by Robin Orr and Dohnányi. Eventually Emanuel Hurwitz replaced Maria and when we added the pianist Edith Vogel and later James Gibb to the ensemble we were known as The London Piano Quartet. "Mannie" Hurwitz proved to be a most inspiring leader, with great vitality and possessing the art of turning a phrase in a most affecting manner. He is one of the most respected chamber musicians that Britain has produced and was duly honoured in 1965 when he received the Worshipful Company of Musicians' Gold Medal for Outstanding Services to Chamber Music.

I would also like to say a few words about my dear and valued friend James Gibb. Sitting around a table at a meeting of the Society for the Promotion of New Music, I noticed that my immediate neighbour had a book of letters by Robert Burns beside him. In conversation with him afterwards I mentioned the fact that I didn't know that Burns had written anything except poetry. He quickly put me right; 'the letters are marvellous' he said, 'just as fascinating as the poems'. The letters were unfortunately out of print in this country but I eventually ran them to ground in Athens!

Jimmy joined the London Piano Quartet in the early fifties and proved to be a great asset. We played many concerts together and broadcast frequently. He is an avid reader and has a huge collection of books. He has a host of friends in many countries and stays often with us, which is always a joy and something we never fail to look forward to. Apart from his talent as a pianist, he is a very erudite speaker and his comments on music and personalities are most revealing, but kindly. Jimmy also has a delightfully bawdy sense of humour and a fund of stories to keep us amused. He is Head of the Piano Department at The Guildhall School of Music, a keen gourmet and a knowledgeable ornithologist. How he finds time to indulge all his whims and fancies is always a mystery. What an entertaining friend to have!

The Aeolian String Quartet, the London String Trio and The London Piano Quartet, together with occasional solo engagements, kept me fully occupied for a number of years, with concerts throughout the length and breadth of the country, broadcasting and recording. With the help of my wife Mary, I did all the correspondence, arrangement of rehearsals and business matters relating to these groups and also much writing of programme notes for concerts. I would often work a seven day week, starting at 9.00 am and not finishing until very late at night. Nevertheless the schedule seemed to suit me as I never missed a single engagement through all these years. Holidays were rare events and often had to be sacrificed in the interests of work. This caused a big strain on my private life and my marriage was destined to end in divorce. Mary and I had grown apart; we had been through difficult times both financially and emotionally but had somehow managed to survive. However, indifference had crept into our relationship, and as our two boys were now ready to leave home for university, it was time to consider separation. It was not a sudden decision, but one to which I had come with much regret and sadness and a great deal of heart-searching over the years.

During that period I met Jean Beckwith who was in time to become my second wife and an ideal partner through the second half of my life. Thus I acquired three stepsons all with artistic bents. Michael the eldest has become a poet; Philip is a sculptor and Gerald, the youngest and in many ways the most musical.

Chapter 7

Solo Playing and Teaching

Throughout my professional career I was always busy as a soloist and always on the look out for new works to add to the limited viola repertoire. On many happy occasions I was partnered by my good friend Myers Foggin and together we gave the first public performance of Richard H. Walthew's Sonata in D at Conway Hall. Some months before, Decca had invited us to record this work, my first solo recording, which we coupled with the composer's *Mosaic in four pieces*. We also recorded my transcription of Schubert's *Arpeggione* Sonata and made the first recording of the demanding Bliss Sonata, with much help and encouragement from the composer. For Decca I also recorded the Bax *Fantasy* Sonata and *Two Folk Songs* by William Alwyn with the harpist Maria Korchinska.

Broadcasting soon became important to me and I gave many sonata recitals for the BBC, often featuring new music. Myers Foggin and I gave the first broadcast performance of Walter Leigh's delightful *Sonatina*, and from Bristol during the war I broadcast the *Dale Romance* with Benjamin Dale at the piano. This live broadcast was at 4.00 am and I remember Dale remarking about the nightingales singing on our way up to the studio.

I have always had a keen interest in arranging music for my instrument, and the poor classical repertoire for the viola has certainly fostered this. So naturally I was interested when the Light Programme of the BBC asked for small ensembles to play light music in half-hour stints. Being a viola player, my ensemble had to be somewhat esoteric, and I formed the Keltic Trio—spelt with a K to indicate that it was not truly Celtic in intent. I asked Alan Richardson, as pianist/composer, and William Alwyn as flautist/composer to join with me and our ensemble flourished. All the music had to be specially arranged and we all took a turn. I remember the fun we had trying out our arrangements and chatting about them. It was a fruitful period, and we enjoyed the change to light music. It only came to an end when the Light Programme of the BBC was eventually reorganised and the fashion for this kind of ensemble faded away.

William played the flute in those days, but he eventually gave it up as composition took up more and more of his time. He wrote a number of works for me in my early career, including a *Ballade* for viola and piano that Myers Foggin and I premiered in a RAM New Music Society Concert. In the same programme David Carl Taylor, my colleague from the Stratton Quartet, joined me in Arnold Cooke's new Duo for violin and viola. Two years later William wrote a beautiful *Pastoral Fantasia* for viola and string orchestra. I gave the first performance of the viola and piano version in 1940 with the distinguished pianist Clifford Curzon, and the following year I was the soloist in the premier of the orchestral version with the BBC Symphony Orchestra conducted by Sir Adrian Boult, which was broadcast from the orchestra's wartime home in Bedford.

In the role of soloist with orchestras, I remember giving other first performances, in particular the premiere of the Concerto by John Greenwood at a Henry Wood Promenade Concert in 1956. We later broadcast the work from Manchester, and during the performance there was a slight earth tremor which I never noticed. So often one thing leads to another. Alan Richardson and I played a sonata by Stephen Dodgson at an SPNM concert in the early 1950's and as a consequence the composer invited me to give the first performance of his *Serenade* for solo viola and orchestra with the Royal Philharmonic Orchestra conducted by Walter Goehr.

In the early days of the war, someone asked me to give a concert with Denise Lassimonne; this was right out of the blue. I had heard of Miss Lassimonne as being the adopted daughter of that famous pedagogue of the piano, Tobias Matthay, who had written various books about piano playing and founded a school in Wimpole Street which was world famous. His pupils were numerous, particularly from America where his most celebrated pupil Myra Hess then enjoyed great popularity. Anyhow, Denise Lassimone and I met, rehearsed and gave a very successful concert. My previous partner had been Myers Foggin, but he had recently joined the Forces and so I drifted into a partnership with Denise—a partnership which was to last for several years and was very fruitful. Despite my commitment to the RAF, we were soon broadcasting, recording for Decca and playing at the National Gallery concerts. My chief concern was over repertoire. I had made arrangements of the Bach viola da gamba sonatas and the Schubert *Arpeggione* sonata, and these we played, but I was dismayed to find that modern music was not in Denise's repertoire. However, we did successfully attempt the Bloch Suite and the Hindemith Sonatas with great enthusiasm, and tackled some other modern works as well. Our rehearsals were at my home in London and at Tobias Matthay's house in Haslemere, where we enjoyed the added advantage of playing to the great man himself. He listened to all we had to play and was most helpful in his comments and criticisms.

From this time too sprang my interest in wine. I drank wine, I bought it, I invested in wine and I made wine. It became an abiding hobby and still is. Then, because of Denise's influence, it was French wine only, but later I tasted the joys of German, Italian and particularly Spanish wine. Sherry I adore—if it is dry—all other drinks pale into insignificance by comparison. I can tolerate a dry Martini, also an occasional whisky, but wine, glorious wine, is the favourite lubricant.

At the time I came to know Tobias Matthay he was living in semiretirement; pupils still came and had lessons, and several came to consult him and to play through their recital programmes for his comments. He was surrounded by some of the teachers who had been associated with him in London. Although Matthay was getting on in years, his mind was still lively. He was slightly deaf to voices but his hearing of music was still acute. He could spot wrong notes, wrong balance and untidy ensemble. He had a curious habit of singing a phrase to us by way of illustration—always a semitone sharper than it was played by us—a strange phenomenon which I have noticed in other musicians as they grow older. He tried a hearing aid and one night came down to dinner wearing it, fiddling around with the controls.

The following evening he came down without the aid. On being quizzed about it he confessed that the new toy was uncomfortable but, more to the point, he heard, actually heard, all our conversation and found it so inane that he eventually decided he would rather enjoy silence!

I was finding the meagre repertoire of classical viola music very unrewarding and found myself playing more and more of my own arrangements, some of these in collaboration with Alan Richardson. After the war, Denise Lassimonne was not so available and it seemed only right that I should team up with Alan. So for the next two decades Alan and I worked as a duo, playing at music societies throughout Britain. We collaborated over many arrangements, transcriptions and editions and Alan dedicated a number of works to me. He had a most charming gift for composition, excelling in short pieces. His *Sussex Lullaby* goes so well on the viola that it is difficult to realise it was originally a piano piece. With Myers Foggin I played this at Conway Hall in 1938 and it stayed in my repertoire until I stopped playing the viola very recently. His next viola work was a virtuoso Scottish piece called *Intrada* and we collaborated over the two Scottish Melodies—*The Lea Rig* and *Whaur the Gadie Rins*—which though founded on folk tunes are quite elaborate in their setting. More ambitious was Alan's *Autumn Sketches*, consisting of an Introduction, Air and Seven Variations. The piece is well named since there is music of a quiet, pastoral, reflective character, varied with strong scenes of much vigour and brilliance. His Sonata Op. 21 is a fine work which has never quite gained the place it deserves in the repertoire. We gave the first performance at Queen Mary Hall, London, and also the first broadcast. There is much to admire in the first movement with its well worked out manipulation and development of the themes. The Scherzo is fast and light-footed—a brilliant piece of writing for both instruments. This is followed by a rhapsodic slow movement and a most satisfying finale. In dedicating the work to me, Alan wrote "This is to commemorate many happy occasions and twenty years hard work. Let's look forward to the next twenty with the hope of Spring eternal." This style of music is at the moment out of fashion, being tuneful and comparatively easy to enjoy. I am in no doubt that it will return, and in time have a most happy revival.

Our duo repertoire included a large and substantial part of the standard repertoire, plus many works by living composers especially written for us, as well as our transcriptions and arrangements. We premiered Robin Orr's Sonata at a concert in Cambridge in 1947 and worked closely with the composer at every stage of the composition. After a short Introduction which has some very effective double stopping, the main part of the first movement is an intricately constructed fugue, the subject announced by the viola being answered a semitone higher by the piano. Six succeeding entries, each a semitone higher, and each in decorated form, complete the exposition. The climax toward the end shows the subject in augmented form, and later there are entries in stretto. The Elegy consists of a long cantabile melody for the viola and the Scherzetto alternates rhythmic pizzicato chords and running quavers. A brisk and contrapuntal movement completes the work. This finale is episodic, with something of the characteristic of rondo form. I well recall the various episodes—each on separate sheets of manuscript paper—lying around my studio while the composer tried to make up his mind as to the sequence of events. Playing the movement through there is no trace of indecision, on the contrary, it all seems so much of a piece that the ideas seem to follow an inevitable sequence. This is exciting music, but it is also intellectually stimulating; the product of a profound musical mind.

Alan and I included two works by another Scottish composer, Norman Fulton, in our repertoire. His *Introduction, Air and Reel* which is dedicated to me, was written in 1950. This is powerful music with a grand sweep to it. His later *Sonata da Camera* is a compact work in three movements; the lively first is followed by a thoughtful slow movement and a lazy paced humorous finale.

I must mention two works by other composers: one by Berkeley which is well known to viola players, and the other by the late Kenneth Leighton which is less familiar.

Lennox Berkeley studied at Oxford and then in France with the late Nadia Boulanger during the period 1927-33. The French influence is usually noticeable in his music, particularly in his early compositions where it is combined with a youthful appeal. It is melodious and fairly diatonic with enough individuality to give it lasting qualities. I instance the popular String Trio and also the Viola Sonata which he wrote for me in 1945. He was very definitely attracted to the viola—its slightly veiled sound, its still unplumbed depths—and I distinctly remember him telling me that soon after the introduction he was going to write a descending scale down to a particularly rich effect on the C string. And there it is, *con colore!* The extended first movement has many dramatic moments using passage work and double-stopping to gain effect. The slow movement is a real adagio, meditative and slow moving. I remember Berkeley telling me that the last movement was giving him some trouble, and how aghast he was when walking along Wigmore Street he saw on bills outside the Wigmore Hall: 'Sonata, Ist Performance, by Lennox Berkeley'. 'Heavens! I haven't got a last movement yet!' And so it was written in haste and, behold, it has all the freshness and wit of real spontaneity, the changing time signatures adding piquancy to the music. This music has retained a pleasing popularity with viola players.

Many composers have written works taking as the subject matter the letters B-A-C-H (German for B-flat, A, C, B-natural). One of the most interesting is the *Fantasia*, Op. 29 by Kenneth Leighton, written in 1955. Leighton, after his training at Oxford, went to Rome to study with Petrassi; this period was to have a continuing influence on his work in the years ahead. A prolific composer, he wrote a great deal of chamber music and also some beautifully effective music for voices. As a nation we tend to neglect our own composers, and they are slow in gaining recognition abroad. Leighton's *Fantasia* for viola should be in every viola player's repertoire. Let me say straight away it is not easy and ensemble with the piano has its problems, but it is effective in performance. The opening adagio is followed by a vigorous allegro, both sections having some involved rhythmic problems. A chorale and a final fugue complete this most invigorating work. Kenneth Leighton and I gave the first performance of this work at an SPNM concert.

I had kept up a tenuous relationship with the Royal Academy of Music since I ceased to be a student in 1932. I had been elected a Fellow in the late forties and from time to time was asked to adjudicate for prizes, but it was not until the mid-fifties that I became Professor of Chamber

Music. I had enjoyed some interesting experiences in teaching as a sub–professor during my student days, and might have graduated into a full professorship at the end of my tuition if I had been keen on the idea, but I was determined to play and to devote all my time and energies to playing while I was young thereby gaining the experience I could pass on to my pupils in due course. I had no regrets when I saw how some of my erstwhile student colleagues, who had elected to stay on as professors, had become quite moribund and undistinguished in their teaching.

Teaching is an honourable profession and a very vital one but I believe in the old adage—play while you can, and teach when you must! When I left the Academy the order of the day was to play wherever one could earn an honest penny: jazz bands, Vaudeville, commercial recordings, orchestras and later on film music, these were all grist to my mill. But all the time I kept my sights on serious music, playing solos, and practising hard. I played quartets and rehearsed assiduously. It was a hard life, compared with which the life of a Roman galley slave seemed desirable. But later on in life, on coming back to teach, I had experienced most things and was ready to share all I had learnt.

My time was now divided between solo playing, chamber music and teaching—no more orchestral playing or commercial work. I still found time to do some arrangements and a modicum of adjudication and examining—the latter happily falling due during the vacations of teaching. It was a stringent life financially, but a happy and interesting one, despite the fact that the income from the RAM was quite miserable—even disgraceful—the attitude being that it was an honour to be associated with such an august institution.

Two years after my appointment as Professor of Chamber Music I was asked to take on viola pupils, which delighted me, particularly as there appeared to be a very talented array of students, some of whom were later to occupy key positions in chamber music ensembles and orchestras.

It was a busy life, and in order to send my two sons to a decent school a seven day working week was required. This frequently meant starting at 9.00.a.m. and not finishing until late at night. A workaholic if you like, but nevertheless the schedule seemed to suit me as I never missed a single engagement throughout all these years. Holidays were rare events and often had to be sacrificed in the interests of work. So now, in retirement, holidays are prized and much appreciated as recompense for past hard labour.

During this time some appointments came my way which were very gratifying, such as Warden of the Solo Performers Section of the Incorporated Society of Musicians. I also became a member of the Music Committee of the Arts Council.

Teaching was a new challenge, and at the Academy I found working with students often most stimulating. I had to assess both their needs and their capabilities, for I did not believe in foisting a 'method' on them automatically. The main lack I found in the average student was a lack of style—they arrived emotionally filleted—but whether this was due to the 'stiff–upper–lip' type of schooling or the inarticulateness of youth it was difficult to say. They tended to be shy and inexpressive and my chief task was to rouse them and give them a feeling for style embracing the whole picture of the artist in relation to performance—deportment, stance, graciousness in acknowledging applause, the re-creation of music in terms of the period in which the composer lived—more by suggestion than by fidelity to physical detail. While it is certainly interesting, for instance, to play Bach's unaccompanied string works on period instruments, it is not, in my opinion, essential for musical veracity.

I encouraged students to build their own library of scores and continually stressed the value of self–discipline and vigilance in never neglecting the daily practice, however busy or tired they were professionally The competition is so fierce that you cannot afford to neglect your technical equipment.

Between the wars there had been some excellent chamber music at the Academy; in the 1920s under the direction of Lionel Tertis, but it was somewhat in disarray when I took it over. I shared the task with my old friend Gwynne Edwards and we soon brought some discipline into the proceedings. Our main task was to supply well–prepared performances for the chamber concerts which took place about three times a term. We found a reluctance to tackle anything in any way contemporary, but I think we did quite a great deal to break down this prejudice. At first the repertoire included works by Haydn, Mozart, early Schubert, Dvořák, and some of the mature Beethoven works with the more advanced players, but little by little the repertoire widened to include works by Schoenberg, Stravinsky, Webern, Hindemith, Bartók, Messiaen and all the major figures in British music at the time, such as Rawsthorne, Britten, Tippett, Bliss, Walton, and many of the younger composers like Hugh Wood, Richard Stoker, David Lyon and Timothy Baxter.

My humble ambition when I became Head of Chamber Music at the Royal Academy was to foster chamber music playing in such a way that I would have students who would play chamber music for a living. Ultimately I wished to form a string quartet that would stay together after the students left the Academy, in much the same way that the Griller String Quartet had accomplished in the 1920s. I managed to fulfil my first ambition through a number of highly talented students who later established themselves as major figures in the chamber music scene. I achieved my second ambition by launching two string quartets—the Alberni and the Lindsay. The Alberni Quartet was appointed resident quartet in Harlow, and the Lindsay Quartet took up a similar post at Keele University. Both quartets flourish to this day.

Throughout my professional career I also gave private lessons and consultations to amateur, student and professional players and undertook chamber music and orchestral coaching at many weekend and summer school courses, including Downe House where I was Director of Chamber Music for many years. I held a similar position in Gloucestershire for the annual courses held at Cowley Manor and Cirencester Agricultural College. At the latter I had great help and assistance from the County Music Adviser, Bob Clifford, and from the late Tony Hewitt Jones. One rewarding aspect of these courses was the opportunity I had to develop my skills as a conductor, an activity in which I continue to find considerable pleasure to this day.

Chapter 8

Violas and Viola Players

If anyone had asked me at an early stage of my career (nobody did!) what my aim was, I would have replied, "To be as successful a viola player as my talent permits, and a dedicated musician, after which, if you insist, health, wealth and happiness." "health abounding, wealth in moderation and happiness as and where it can be found." Happiness, not to be confused with pleasure, though the two are often conjoined. I hadn't much time for St.Paul's Faith, Hope and Charity, except if charity is translated as love and especially if love means loving kindness and a degree of tolerance. If anybody had asked me what my ambitions, as opposed to my aims, were, (and again nobody did) I would have replied, "Work, Philosophy and String Quartets". This trinity of ideas has not changed much over the years, except that my interest in String Quartets has ceased to be paramount now that I no longer play them. I would substitute listening to music, though my taste is hardly catholic. If only I enjoyed listening as much as playing! But in the end, it all comes back to the viola, and it must be pretty plain to anyone who has the patience to read this rigmarole that there is no doubt the viola is definitely my first choice.

As a student of the violin I had been bothered over notes in the higher register. The trouble was not so much that I had difficulty in reaching them or pitching them, as a distaste for the sound of them. The tessitura was always uncomfortable. As soon as I changed to the viola I was suddenly at ease over pitch. The viola is not suited, in my opinion, to soar upwards with the ease and glory of the cello, but is better suited to a more modest register. I have played the viola every day, yes, even into my eighties; and despite occasional trouble with arthritis, it has given me a thrill every time I have taken it up. I have played on a Stradivarius, a Guidantus and a Guadagnini; I have had violas made for me by Colin Irving, Arthur Richardson, Rex England and William Luff—those made by the latter two I prize especially. I have encouraged composers to write works for me, with commendable results. I have arranged or edited literally hundreds of works for the viola and I am still adding to the list. In fact, I am a viola maniac!

My first really good instrument was a viola by Guidantus, beautiful to look at and in many ways very good as a performing instrument but it lacked a little in depth of tone. I had been badgering W. E. Hill & Sons for a better instrument for several years before they told me about a Guadagnini, made in Turin during his later period and dated 1775. I agreed to have it, only to find that many of the viola players in London were after it. I had to borrow the money from my father, which I did with a promise to pay in instalments as and when I had accumulated the cash but this agreement my father refused. In its place he asked me to pay him ten shillings (fifty pence) per week from the day he retired until he died. His weekly outlay was modest, an occasional packet of cigarettes and a flutter on the horses from time to time so I immediately agreed, thinking I had struck a bargain. Well, he was sixty–nine years old when he retired and he lived until he was ninety–two, and every week I paid him his ten shillings! So who was laughing all the way to the bank?

The Guadagnini was a handy size, 16" in body length but having a fine contralto quality of tone, somewhat on the dark side but carrying well. At that time there was a vogue for playing on extra large violas giving forth a cello quality of sound. These varied from 17" to 18" in body length but many players strained their arms and shoulders trying to play on these gigantic instruments. I stuck to my own ideal of production. In fact I have often found that violas of even smaller dimensions than those I favoured—meaning about 14½" to 15½" had attractive features of sweetness of tone and ease of response quite denied to these monstrous instruments. When, in the fullness of time, the Royal Academy of Music lent me the Archinto Strad of 1696, I laid the Guadagnini aside and played for ten years on the

Strad. The instrument was very responsive, if inclined to be temperamental, with a slightly soprano quality of tone, but at its best a great joy to play, and oh, how beautiful to behold! I often took it out of its case and laid it on a table, just to admire the beauty and symmetry of its design and the glowing colour of its varnish. I returned the Strad to the Academy as the qualities of the Guadagnini were more and more demanded in the Quartet. I was sorry to part with it, it had become so very much part of me. I played on the Guadagnini for the next twenty years.

Then my serious playing days were over and I felt I must part with it to a more active player. In the meantime I had played on a violin made by William Luff, the property of Trevor Williams. I hadn't played a violin since my student days! I liked the borrowed Luff fiddle so much I asked him to make one for me; this he did, and a grand instrument it turned out to be, a copy of the Heifetz *Guarnerius del Gesu.*

Before I parted with my Guadagnini viola, I had a copy made. Who but Luff to make it? A charming, old–fashioned, courteous man to deal with. I showed him the viola and off he went to see if he could match the wood. One day he rang up in a tremendous state of excitement to say that after a long search he had eventually gone up into his attic where, to his delight, he found a piece of wood which was practically a replica of the one piece back, even to a small knot in the wood! After this he couldn't wait to get his hands on my original Guadagnini so one day when we were flying off for a holiday, I handed my precious viola over to him in—of all places—the lounge of the airport terminal at Victoria station! He had brought the piece of wood up to London with him, so there and then, he felt he must compare the two. Out came the viola from its case and Luff's eyes lit up as he saw it was going to work—all this to the astonishment of the bystanders.

So off we went on our holiday, and on our return he had the copy made. I could hardly tell which was the real Guadagnini and which the copy, they looked so very much alike; not only that, they sounded alike. With her back turned towards me, my wife Jean couldn't tell which was which—we were delighted.

After I had played the new viola for some time I was ready to sell the Guadagnini (not without a pang). I took it to Phillips for their autumn sale. After the sales assistant had told me what he thought of the instrument—"What a pity it's been re-varnished, and look at this knot in the back, and of course it isn't the original scroll"—I said humbly, "By the way, it makes a beautiful sound". He practically ignored this remark so that I began to wonder if I had an instrument of any value whatsoever! To my complete astonishment after this unpropitious start, he then suggested putting a reserve of £8,000 on it! The instrument sold for £18,000!

I was examining one day the pupils of an enthusiastic teacher, and during the course of the morning she offered to show me her viola (not her etchings) and produced a fine, new and well made instrument with a rich bold tone. It had been made by a local man, a school teacher who had in fact also made several of the violins on which her pupils had played. I said I would like to meet him, if it were possible, and so I made the acquaintance of Rex England, a most interesting and enthusiastic craftsman. I immediately ordered a violin, which I still have pleasure in playing. I collected it from him in the refreshment room at Euston station where he arrived carrying the instrument in a Marks and Spencer's bag! Strange how my instrumental transactions seem to take place in railway stations!

Later, I asked Rex England to make me another copy of my late Guadagnini but he refused, saying he preferred to keep to the Hoing–designed model to which he was accustomed. The viola proved to be too large for me, especially in the stop. He later made a copy of an Amati, barely 16", which I took to immediately. It has a full tone and a glorious sound on the lower strings; I adored it and very much enjoyed playing on it, but my favourite instrument is still the Luff copy of my Guadagnini.

Meantime, I had still a hankering after the Guadagnini model and coaxed Colin Irving to make me a more or less accurate copy. It turned out to be a most handsome instrument with a very full tone, a little on the brash side, it has somewhat mellowed with the passing years, but is an excellent viola for those who wish to play concertos, for it would cut through any orchestra without undue pressure. I also had a violin made by Martin Hilsden, beautifully fashioned, which has also matured well. I had got the craze for collecting fiddles and would have continued ad lib, had Jean not protested loudly saying, "After all, you can only play on one instrument at a time, why so many?" Of course, reluctantly, I had to own that she was right, and with increasing age I have sold some of my collection. Others I am loath to part with—but shall do so in the fullness of time.

With so many instruments passing through my hands, one might assume that I have a profound knowledge of the fine points of violin and viola making, but this would be far from the truth. I value a fiddle purely by how it sounds, whether it is in a healthy condition, and whether it is tolerably easy to handle. I am amazed when a dealer can, at a glance give the name of the maker, the year it was made, all in the twinkling of an eye. Though I can be impressed by the look of an instrument and appreciate the beauty of design and varnish, I value the instrument not by the name on the label, but purely from its desirability to me as a performer.

Colossal sums of money are invested in violins by celebrated makers without more than a passing evaluation of their tonal qualities. The young viola player or violinist embarking on a career has to make up his mind as to what he requires from his fiddle. When instruments are tested, old against new, the new invariably comes off best; I have myself tested fiddles in this way and have often favoured the new model. So you wish to buy one as an investment, or as a vehicle for your performance? Perhaps you wish to have your cake and eat it—a valuable old instrument which is fun to perform on. Whatever you decide, do realise that you and your playing are the essential features. Only about five per cent is due to the instrument. "You" will always sound like "you"; your sound is as intimately "you" as your signature—or even more so!

The making of bows is generally a separate art form. Few violin makers make bows. From my student days I collected them, not antique ones, but new bows, generally from the workshops of W. E. Hill & Son (then of Bond Street but later of Great Missenden). Their bows suited me very well indeed. I paid fifteen guineas for them and have sold some of them, later in life, for most inflated prices. One, reputedly made by Tubbs, cost me eighteen guineas. I never liked the bow but admired the workmanship very much indeed and this has sold for an astronomical sum, not just hundreds of pounds, but thousands.

Hill's had a fine crowd of craftsmen in their works at that time. Becoming tired of the anonymity of having their bows branded 'Hill & Sons', some of these men branched out on their own. One of these, Arthur Bultitude, I decided to contact. He lived in the country and continued to make excellent bows until old age caught up with him. I went on a voyage of discovery, and finally ran him to earth in a shed in his garden, working away at his craft.

I was intrigued by the fact that his emblem in the nut was not, as Hills always favoured, a fleur–de–lys, but an English rose. I suddenly thought, and suggested to him, that he should make a Scottish thistle instead, and thus was born an emblem under which he produced many of his finest bows.

My final purchase during my professional life was from a player who had gone over to jazz. For this bow I paid £27 and suffered many sleepless nights thereafter, being quite certain that I had been diddled into paying too much It became my favourite bow and must now be worth a fortune.

Chapter 9

Head of Music, BBC, Scotland

As we approached 1962 I realised that I had been a member of the string quartet for thirty years; I began to feel restive, longing for a change of scene. What else could I do? I could administer or conduct.

I had had experience of administration looking after the various ensembles—no easy task; my conducting experience was limited, but reasonably successful. What prompted the desire for a change? Although everything seemed to be ticking over nicely I was bored. I was tired of the compulsory practising, fed up with incessant rehearsals with the same problems being encountered day after day. I was in danger of getting into a rut. During all my years in the Aeolian Quartet, I only ever missed one performance. We had agreed to give a charity concert and perform for no fee. I was unwell but we couldn't easily withdraw our services, so I had to pay for a deputy! There is a moral to be found somewhere in this story, but I find it difficult to disentangle! Now, I wished for new challenges before I became too old and senile, or settled, to meet them. I kept my eyes and ears open for another two years, and when finally the solution stared me in the face, I didn't at first realise it, but went off for a boating holiday on the canals instead.

Trevor Williams, who was at that time leader of the BBC Scottish Orchestra, wrote to tell me that the post of Head of Music, BBC, Scotland, was vacant and begged me to apply. He said I was just the man for the job! I discussed the idea with my wife Jean and wondered if, after all the years in London, I really wanted to return to Scotland. If I got the position it would mean having to retire from the various ensembles, from my Professorship at the RAM—in fact, a complete change of life. In a way just what I wanted... and yet... To cut a long story short, we decide I should apply and after all, if I were chosen, I could still refuse. I applied, was short–listed, and against stiff local opposition was offered the job.

Before leaving for Scotland I had an interview with Sir Thomas Armstrong, Principal of the RAM, and resigned my position there. He was most interesting in his comments. He said that in all the major changes in his life he had rarely achieved his ambitions but nevertheless, had always been awarded positions which in the end turned out better than his own ideas. (Determinism versus Free Will?) He made a speech of farewell at one of the Academy concerts that was almost embarrassing in its fulsome assessment of my work at the Academy.

Saying goodbye to the quartet was not easy after so many years of good comradeship and hard labour—after all, we were in the middle of a well booked season and presently committed to playing all the Bartók quartets in a series. Choosing my successor was also no easy task. We had always been an all male organisation, except for a brief period during the war, and all possible players seemed to be fully booked. Eventually Jean said, 'What about Margaret Major?'. We had been to a recital of hers some time before and had been most impressed by her playing. So she was approached, she accepted, and proved to be a most worthy and successful successor .

Scotland was indeed a change. No more practising, no more rehearsals, no more teaching, no more examining! At the BBC there were two orchestras resident in Glasgow, the BBC Scottish Orchestra under its conductor Norman del Mar and a light dance orchestra under its conductor Jack Leon. There were chamber music concerts, solo recitals, and the organisation of bagpipe programmes, as well as Scottish dance music. Of course, I had devoted and hard working assistants in all these departments.

The BBC Scottish Choral Society had fallen on hard times and, I suppose, could have been immediately disbanded, but I felt that a rescue was more to the point. We even appealed on the radio for tenors—some of the public thought we were asking for tenners—but had no success in either direction. Gradually, however, the Society got on its feet once more and went on to give some splendid broadcasts.

Being a member of a committee seemed to me often to be a colossal bore—a recipe for inaction—but having no particular axe to grind, those I served on in Scotland were quite enjoyable. The Edinburgh Festival Committee and the Scottish Archive both did useful work. I had been appointed to my position by the Scottish Broadcasting Council and so had to report to that committee on my activities from time to time. It was good to be in the happy position of being able to report on a growing awareness of music by Scottish composers and Scottish performers, both vocal and instrumental. There was sometimes difficulty in deciding who was to be considered Scottish so I cast my net wide and include in our programmes not only those who were Scottish by descent but also those musicians who had settled in Scotland and contributed substantially to the Scottish scene. I aimed to have programmes which included a work by a Scottish composer, or a programme presented by a Scottish performer (or, indeed, both). Eventually this succeeded in unearthing a great deal of native talent eager to participate and which only required encouragement to come alive.

Amidst an atmosphere of new confidence we were lucky to find money to expand the BBC Scottish Orchestra with extra strings and also a fifth horn, and presently the orchestra had the satisfaction of adding 'Symphony' to its title, which was a truer expression of its nature. During our first few months in Glasgow the orchestra was conducted by Norman del Mar who was most helpful and friendly to me in every way, but, my word, how his natural exuberance exhausted the orchestra. He had peculiarly small feet for a man of his size and a habit of leaping vertically off the rostrum when particularly excited. One wondered how such very small feet could bear the landing impact of such a large man. He was a music-aholic and even the bookcase in his lavatory was full of miniature scores instead of the customary offerings. On returning to London he was replaced by James Loughran.

Jimmy had flair, real musical flair. A little raw and inexperienced to begin with, he soon showed the qualities that were to see him on to greater heights and become a conductor of world-wide significance. Our collaboration and discussions were most enjoyable and we are friends to this day. It must have come as quite a surprise to him after our five harmonious years together when he found his contract was not to be renewed. I think he felt he was settled with the BBC Scottish Orchestra for life. I tactfully suggested that he was worthy to move on to more significant and important work further afield. Eventually he came to discuss three possibilities with me—two of them abroad and the third on home ground, the Hallé Orchestra in Manchester. I favoured the Hallé and it was there that he went, in succession to Sir John Barbirolli. It was not such a good orchestra as he was leaving but full of opportunity, of which he made the most.

His place was taken by Christopher Seaman. This young man had progressed from being assistant conductor to James Loughran. This was an admirable scheme run by the Scottish Broadcasting Council whereby a young hopeful conductor was given a two–year engagement to conduct a certain number of concerts and given free rein to do what he could on his own with only the minimum control in matters of repertoire and technique. It was a challenge from which emerged several well–known conductors. Seaman's elevation to chief conductor was a popular choice with the orchestra, with whom he enjoyed a great rapport and it gave me the opportunity to appoint Andrew Davis as assistant conductor. This mercurial musician enjoyed a rapid rise to fame, quickly establishing his position as a conductor of note and going on to international success. I think he 'found himself' during his apprenticeship in Scotland. Not an easy man to handle, but always interesting and exciting to work with!

It was a great joy and good fortune to have Trevor Williams as leader of the orchestra. He was greatly respected by the orchestra with whom he occasionally played concertos—I remember him giving a particularly fine performance of the Walton Concerto. Unfortunately for us in Scotland, William Glock, Head of Music, BBC, London cast a covetous eye on him as possible leader of the BBC Symphony Orchestra. Much as I was reluctant to release him, I felt I couldn't stand in his way as it meant promotion and a great challenge for him. We had many a chat about this change in his fortunes before he decided to go. He was succeeded for a short time by Leonard Friedman, and then by Tom Rowlette who served the orchestra magnificently for six years.

I had invited Sydney Humphreys, who had retired from the Aeolian String Quartet and gone home to Canada, to play concertos with the orchestra whenever he visited Britain, and these performances he fulfilled with distinction. After one of his performances I was puzzling as to who should succeed Tom Rowlette, who had been forced to retire through ill health, and mentioned this dilemma to Sydney. To my great surprise and delight he said, "What about me?". To have a player of this distinction was indeed a feather in our caps; only one thing slightly worried me. Sydney had never played in an orchestra; the discipline was foreign to him, the repertoire unknown. Would he succeed in overcoming these handicaps? I needn't have worried. He succeeded even beyond our expectations and became a vital force in the orchestra. He studied orchestral scores, he borrowed recordings, he even went to sleep with the sound of music plugged into his ear. It was indeed a happy fulfilment of all my hopes for the orchestra.

There are two other musicians in the orchestra who simply cannot go unmentioned, both having been founder members in 1935. Sanchia Pilau, the harpiste, was a most lively Irish lady and a distinguished performer. She had an identical twin sister living in New Zealand and told us many tales of the simultaneity of idea and even of dress that they both had at this great distance. As member of the Buchanan Ensemble (of which more later) she took part in many of our concerts and gave delightful performances of the Debussy Sonata for flute harp and viola. Until her death in 1993 she was in great demand as teacher and player.

Another remarkable musician was John McInulty, the very distinguished leader of the cello section. John was particularly noted for his beautiful tone production which was full, distinctive and individual. I had encouraged players in the orchestra to play concertos, but had trouble with John who was having difficulty with the first finger of his left hand, where pressure on the string had worn a groove which could become quite painful under duress. So we called on our friend, the eminent hand surgeon Athol Parkes, who quickly solved the difficulty by telling John to put a stalwart piece of plaster round the offending finger. It worked well, and was certainly the simplest operation Athol had ever performed. After this John performed several concertos with the orchestra with great distinction, including a fine performance of Don Quixote which elicited congratulations from the BBC in London. Shortly after his retirement, John McInulty was awarded the MBE, and after he died the John McInulty Prize was created to help train string players for orchestral work.

We had many outstanding visiting conductors. Sir Adrian Boult was always a joy to receive, even in old age. His performances were always alert and lively and he had an easy rapport with the orchestra. He was a most impressive figure and his visits were certainly mutually enjoyed. We had both him and his wife to lunch and having heard of his strict non-alcoholic habits and peculiarities of diet we were prepared with plenty of milk and soup, but only to find that he never ate and drank at the same time. These were but minor difficulties however, for they were both most charming and genial guests.

The other conductor I feel must be mentioned, who visited us many times was Rudolf Schwartz. Many years previously my wife, who was a singer, had lessons from him when she lived in Germany. He was delightful company, warm and quiet. Being a Jew in Hitler's Germany he was eventually rounded up and sent to many concentration camps. The brutal treatment he received left him unable to raise his arms above shoulder level which contributed to his personal style of conducting. Some highly placed "angel" must have been protecting him for each time he was due to go to the gas chamber he was sent on to another camp. After the war he made his recovery in a hospital in Sweden and subsequently settled in England where his first appointment was with the Bournemouth Symphony Orchestra. He had a wonderful philosophy of life and despite his trials and tribulations he appeared to bear no rancour towards his tormentors. It was always a joy to welcome him to Scotland. His was surely one of the finest conductors of Mozart and we still recall his outstanding rendering of the Jupiter Symphony.

The celebrated violinist Ida Haendel made regular appearances as a soloist. She became a close friend of the family and on one occasion, after her concert at the Edinburgh Festival, she came and stayed the week-end with us in Loch Goil, meeting my ageing parents, radiating charm, and entertaining us with accounts of her travels and adventures all over the world. No one could have been more simple or charming. Our neighbours, the Morrison Dunbars, visited us and Morrison played a trio sonata with Ida during which, much to our amusement, she almost went astray. She confessed to finding the strain of touring as virtuoso violinist a rather lonely business, just one hotel after another, so that she greatly welcomed being treated as one of the family.

She is a natural fiddler despite her thin delicate hands. She has a lovely and inspired tone production and a quite formidable technique; not for her hour after hour of practice. Once on visiting Heifetz in America, she was invited to his studio to hear a new student play one of the more difficult violin concertos. Before he started he was asked by Heifetz to play the scale of F sharp minor in thirds. This request completely shook the student, who floundered his way through the scale with difficulty. Heifetz turning to Ida said: "Miss Haendel, I'm sure, practises scales daily as the foundation of technique". Completely unabashed, Ida replied that she never practised scales. Later she told me that she only knew a few of the studies by Kreutzer, Rode and Dont, generally regarded as the foundation of a reliable technique. She is indeed a great artist and a very true friend.

The BBC in London had sponsored two competitions for violinists and one for cellists, but when I ventured to suggest that we might have a competition for viola players they immediately turned it down. I had no option but to run the competition myself from Scotland. It was arranged as part of the celebrations which the City of Glasgow organised in honour of her native–born viola virtuoso, William Primrose and so in the teeth of opposition the scheme was launched and the response was absolutely grand. I had Frederick Riddle and Gwynne Edwards to help me judge the preliminary rounds.

I then approached the Lord Provost about arrangements for inviting William Primrose to adjudicate the finals. He was most compliant and very interested. The City Council kindly footed the bill for bringing Primrose from America and for paying his expenses. I wanted them to present him with the Freedom of the City, but they temporised by giving him an official lunch—if only he had been a football player it would have been easy to arrange! BBC Scotland also gave an official lunch and I interviewed him for Radio Scotland. We did our best to honour him and give him first class treatment, and he was obviously absolutely delighted. In fact, as I learned later, this episode in his career set him off on a new venture—a most profitable one—since he was in constant demand from that time forth as adjudicator and lecturer.

Although stationed in Glasgow, my brief was to take music to the whole of Scotland. As Head of Music, I travelled the length and breadth of the country. From time to time we ventured to take the BBC Scottish Symphony Orchestra out of the studio for a festival concert. On one occasion we had the actor Andrew Cruickshank (well known by the general public as Dr Cameron in the first TV series of Dr Finlay's Case Book) to recite with the orchestra. He was a towering personality, with a splendid voice and such a delightful, pawky sense of humour.

On another occasion there was an opportunity for me to accompany a group of six or seven musicians on a visit to Lerwick in the Shetland Isles to introduce their concert. It was one of a series of broadcasts from historic places, the local public being invited to attend. We flew from Glasgow, catching the local plane for the latter part of the journey. We unfortunately ran into fog and had to spend the night in Kirkwall. We arrived in Lerwick just in time for the afternoon balance test and rehearsal, which didn't leave us much time to change into our evening togs and assemble at the local village hall for the concert. This went off splendidly but, unfortunately, as so often happens, the concert coincided with the evening meal at the hotel. We arrived back, ravenous, to find blank faces and no dinner. The only place, apparently were we could get anything to eat was on the pier where there was a fish and chip wagon. So off we set and there was the wagon, and there too, presently, a hungry octet of musicians being served fish and chips in old newspaper; and was it good! We had come straight from the concert and were therefore still in full evening dress and made an incongruous sight munching our fish and chips with relish. We were amused to find the locals assembling to view the unusual sight—a larger audience than had turned up for the concert.

The Controller of BBC Scotland when I arrived on the scene was Andrew Stewart who had progressed from being 'Uncle Andrew' in Children's Hour broadcasts and made his way to achieve his position under the austere eye of Sir John Reith. He carried some of the latter's autocracy of manner with him, but I was warned in advance that he could be a difficult man to get on with and had the luck to establish quite quickly an easy rapport with him. If he frowned on some of my more bizarre ideas he could also be pleasantly indulgent and, at times, most co-operative and understanding. He was succeeded by Alistair Milne who only occasionally displayed the assets that were to take him eventually to be Governor general of the BBC. I had the impression that despite his Gaelic language and bagpipe enthusiasm, that he never felt quite at home in Scotland. He left me fairly free to pursue music in my own way and, in this respect, I was happy.

It was fortunate to have arrived at a time of a great period of development of music in Scotland—one could feel the fervour of possible achievement. Scottish music and musicians were coming to the fore and the Edinburgh Festival was maintaining its world-wide renown. Scottish Opera had been established under the inspired directorship of Robin Orr with Peter Hemming as Administrator and Sir Alexander Gibson conducting. Their productions received universal acclaim and it was gratifying to lend the BBC Scottish orchestra for some of their productions.

Robin Orr has been my friend since we were students. Later our paths divided but always came together every now and again, sufficiently often to keep our friendship alive. After being an undergraduate at Cambridge University, he soon became a lecturer there and it was during this period that he wrote his Viola Sonata, a couple of little pieces and a String Trio. Then he returned to Scotland to become Professor of Music at Glasgow University. Although he seemed to have such a flair for organisation, he still kept on writing music and I had great joy in arranging several programmes for the BBC Scottish Symphony Orchestra to broadcast, including his Overture *Prospect of Whitby*, his First Symphony and his Opera *Full Circle*. He responded by dedicating his Second Symphony to the Orchestra. In an age when Scottish composers were coming to the fore, he must be reckoned as Scotland's premier composer and musician.

As fate would have it, soon after I returned to Scotland, Robin was elected Professor of Music at Cambridge University. So once again, as had so often happened in the past, our paths diverged almost as if luck was determined to play Box and Cox with us. That was over twenty years ago and yet, in spite of all, we are still in touch.

But I have digressed. Other music festivals besides Edinburgh were flourishing, such as Stirling and Montrose. Traditional Scottish music in the form of folk song and traditional fiddling were very much to the fore in our programmes. In fact we launched a competition for Scottish fiddling and one hundred and forty players entered! Not all were of the first standard, but the best played off against each other in a final concert in Perth, at which Yehudi Menuhin was the chief adjudicator.

The standard of playing varied quite considerably during the preliminary rounds. Some players missed the true style of Scottish fiddling by playing as they would a Handel Sonata, others had the particular style in their bones but hadn't the technique to do themselves justice, and many were only what can be best described as 'fireside fiddlers'— players who played for the love of the fiddle and the enchantment of the music. One of the latter kind entertained us immensely by arriving with his dog, which he insisted should accompany him into the studio. We explained that this was out of the question, but that we could look after his dog in the listening room where there was a loudspeaker, and where we were recording the performances in case we had any subsequent doubt about the players. He agreed to this, and furthermore dispensed with the piano accompaniment, an acceptable omission quite often traditionally correct. So, with a preliminary Bang–Bang with his foot, off he set on his performance. The dog, we were told, immediately recognised his master's playing and leapt excitedly towards the loud speaker, finally settling down quite happily but listening intently! After the audition we told the old boy he could take his dog into the studio, whereupon he informed us that he had two more tunes he wanted us to hear—we agreed! The spectacle of this old worthy playing away, so full of spirit, with his dog Iying contentedly over his feet and gazing up at his master in adoration, was almost too much for us.

To have Yehudi Menuhin as adjudicator for the final gave the whole scheme a great boost. When I originally 'phoned him at his hotel in Glasgow, I had scarcely outlined the idea before he was brimming over with enthusiasm for the whole scheme. Although the final of the competition was, at that time, several months ahead, we settled the date straight away. As the day of the final concert came nigh, excitement grew to fever heat! The hall was completely sold out three days before the concert was due.

Menuhin arrived the day before, and when he lunched with us he insisted on having haggis to put him in the proper Scottish mood! During lunch I mentioned that several players had made their own fiddles and would like to show these to him He was delighted, and when the opportunity came he straightway met the Scottish fiddlers, evaluating their instruments, and even playing on some of them. Needless to say, the makers were in their seventh heaven, and what Menuhin had said was the talking point over the whisky for months afterwards! He was intrigued at the expertise displayed by the finalists at the concert. Scottish fiddle music demands a particular style of playing and an expert use of the bow, albeit in a country fashion. The style is passed on from father to son and also by the great exponents of the art. Considerable freedom can be displayed when playing the sentimental tunes, while the strathspeys and reels are not only dance music but have an individual tang which is embroidered by free ornamentation and a most infectious rhythm. It was this freedom and rhythm which intrigued Menuhin, these and the sound which these players produced which is entirely indigenous to Scotland and its fiddlers. These qualities were to be discussed by Menuhin in his final speech which he made to the audience before announcing the result of the competition, which incidentally was won by a player from Shetland. This was to be the first of several visits he made to Scotland to renew his acquaintance with Scottish fiddling.

The fiddle has always been associated with Scottish folk music. Even though in more recent times the piano accordion has made a bold attempt to replace the fiddle, in the dance hall the fiddle remains supreme as the ideal expression of this music.

Why the fiddle and not the violin? The name is carried on from a former instrument, pre–dating the invention of the violin and even the viols. The fedylle, probably only having two strings (hence the old adage about having two strings to your bow) was the direct ancestor of the viol and violin. There were other claimants such as the rebec and the crowd, all similar to each other, but the fedylle lingered on into the sixteenth century when the viols took over. The viols were not as popular with the general public, being reserved for the gentry playing more cultivated music. By the late seventeenth century the violin took over from the fedylle in every way, though the name fiddle lingers on, even today.

What of the music these folk played? The bagpipe, though not invented in Scotland, was the first instrument to foster the folk music of Scotland. It has technical limitations but makes a virtue of these shortcomings, lending to the music a strident but heroic sound.

Fiddlers took over much of this bagpipe music and freely adapted it to the newer instrument. A great upsurge in dancing about the beginning of the eighteenth century acted as a spur to this new development. Fiddlers started to compose in the Scottish idiom, which was so successful that it was often difficult to tell the traditional from the newer composition. The violin was treasured for its sharp, penetrating sound, and the players were aided and abetted by a long line of Scottish fiddle makers who had copied the violins by Stainer, and eventually those of Cremonese makers, Stradivarius, Guarnerius, Amati and so on.

The players quickly established the slow air, calling their compositions Lament, Reverie, Elegie, Pastoral and Barcarolle. The Pibroch, an air with variations, was also relished but this tended to remain the property of the bagpipes. They revelled in strathspeys and reels, using a pithy stroke of the bow in its upper half. Mostly they played in the first position, only occasionally venturing further afield. The style of sound was a basic feature of this new music making. While they didn't go out of their way to incorporate the drone notes of the bagpipes, open strings and double stopping enhanced their performances. Scottish fiddling became as indigenous as Scotch whisky and bannocks.

The characteristic sound of their music making was passed down from family to family. The Pibroch, an Air with variations, (thought by quite a number of people to be some strange animal found only on the Scottish moors) was also relished, but this tended to remain the property of the bagpipes.

Who were these composers? For about a hundred years the Gow family dominated the scene. Famous for his playing at balls and assemblies was the eighteenth century Perthshire man, Neil Gow. He published several fine collections of airs, reels and strathspeys. Nathaniel Gow was the best musician of the family; he contributed about a hundred tunes, some very fine and original, and a descendant, David Gow was also a notable composer and wrote a *Nocturne and Capriccio* Op. 31 for me in the mid 1950s.

One of the most remarkable fiddler–composers was the all–rounder, William Marshall whose playing was praised by Robert Burns. He dabbled not only in Scottish fiddle music—he invented the slow strathspey, designed for concert use only—but was also noted for astronomy, architecture and mechanics. The most famous of all these composer–players was J. Scott Skinner. Players abound nowadays but composers are scarce. These players maintain the traditional style of performance, being careful to differentiate between the characteristic features of Shetland and the Western Isles. By far the most popular style is found in Aberdeen, Perth and Banchory where competitions are frequent.

Traditionally these tunes were played unaccompanied, but gradually the piano was incorporated in an easy vamping style. In the slow airs a degree of rubato is essential to convey the sentiment. Forget the bar lines and indulge in freedom of expression. In the faster movements, slurred notes are infrequent and all are freely ornamented in traditional style. Too close a realisation of the written notation tends to kill the spirit of this music, which has to breathe as freely as the mountain air. Indeed, it would cease to flourish without the support of an indigenous folk culture. Long may this be with us.

It was a happy day when the BBC asked John Noble to become Chairman of the Broadcasting Council for Scotland.

For me it was the beginning of a friendship which lasted until his sudden and tragic death some years later. John was an eccentric in the best sense of this appellation and he had very definite ideas about things musical. He was a real power in the affairs of Scotland, being amongst the richest landowners in the country. He had great pleasure in devoting much of his free time to the BBC Music Department, and hardly a week passed without some detailed letter from him to me about the running of it. His writing was atrocious and I had to get my secretary to decipher many of his letters. During his regime there was a definite move from London to disband the BBC Scottish Symphony Orchestra, and it was largely due to John's efforts that it survived.

Jean and I treasured his friendship very much indeed. Most week–ends we were able to get down to our bungalow on Loch Goil and here, practically without fail, each Sunday before lunch we would see his car coming up the drive and John descending, never without some gift of a pheasant or a bottle of delectable wine. Then we would settle down for a most delightful hour of talk. It was possibly on one of these occasions that he and I had the idea of organising an annual week–end in June at his home at Ardkinglas, inviting thirty or forty of his friends to listen to concerts of chamber music. Since his house had twenty–six bedrooms, he was able to house most of his guests who came from far and wide. His wife, Elizabeth, was a marvellous cook and contrived somehow to be a lovely hostess as well as providing delicious suppers for everyone after the concert— quite a remarkable feat!

It was before these week–ends took place that I had formed the Buchanan Ensemble, consisting of players drawn from the BBC Scottish Symphony Orchestra and myself on viola, and it was this ensemble that supplied the backbone of the music–making at Ardkinglas. John asked us to play such a curious collection of pieces that I found myself writing hither and thither, including abroad, for the music. But it was all well worthwhile, for it was great to take part in such a pleasant and ideal atmosphere with such willing and even eager colleagues. The house itself, built by John Noble's grandfather, and most beautifully positioned on the banks of Loch Fyne had been designed by Lorimer, who took the trouble to design the individual candelabra, locks and fireplaces. It was a real treasure trove and a magical place to stay.

Besides the series of concerts we gave for John Noble, we gave several musical evenings for the Duke and Duchess of Argyll at Inveraray Castle. Our first meeting with the Duchess was a bit crazy. Jean and I were bidden to tea at the Castle to discuss the idea. We were met at the front door by the Duchess herself, who invited us in saying, " Excuse me for a short while, I'm just going for my run" - which was at least an unconventional greeting. From the outside the castle, with its many towers and turrets, standing on the shores of Loch Fyne, looks like an illustration from a fairy tale. Inside, the great hall is lofty and beautiful, and there is a glorious library, but the living rooms are small and cosy. The drawing room, in which we gave our concerts had still the same curtains which hung there as far back as the rebellion of 1745, as well as many mementos of bygone days. I arranged with the Duchess that we should give a single concert with the Buchanan Ensemble, and she was so pleased that we repeated this annually for quite a number of years. Our last concert was given by candle light - a tricky operation as, at the slightest draught, the candles flickered, and were in danger of singeing our valuable bows. By this time we had got to know the Duke and Duchess quite well, and they gave us some charming hospitality, the Duke even taking us up to see the salmon run on the Estate. It was a thrilling sight to see them leaping. Inspite of his slight lack of interest in music, the Duke was a marvellous and gracious host. One charming touch in the castle was in the loo, where a notice hung behind the chain reading, "Pull gently sweet Afton".

In 1930 at a critical period of my studentship, the Sir James Caird Travelling Scholarship for music students of Scottish nationality was announced. I was the first Junior Scholar! I mention this again because the wheel had gone full circle, for it was thirty–five years later while still Head of Music BBC Scotland that I was approached by the Secretary of the Caird and asked if I would accept the Chairmanship of the examining body. It was a great honour, and one which I immediately accepted with much pleasure. I held the appointment for the next ten momentous years. I use the qualification 'momentous', since we had most of the young hopefuls of Scotland through our hands, some of whom were to climb to the top of their profession and become famous far and wide throughout the world.

I had with me a distinguished list of examiners: Joan Dickson looked after the strings and had served many years on the Board, James Gibb attracted the pianists, while Duncan Robertson dealt with the very talented array of singers. Herbert Howells was succeeded by David Wilcocks in assessing the composers and finally there was Robert Crawford who was to become Chairman upon my retirement.

Chapter 10

Retiring from the BBC

On returning to Scotland at the age of fifty–five, I felt quite a stranger. Nevertheless we had great kindness bestowed upon us, and a warm feeling of comradeship was displayed by many people, especially in regard to my interest in fostering the native musical talent. This was difficult to bring forth as the Scots are apt to despise any local talent and favour the imported celebrity.

It was in my very early days in the BBC that I met a chap who was to become a lifelong friend. Morrison Dunbar and his beautiful and gifted wife, Sally, are very dear friends and this delightful relationship is most flattering, as they are many years younger than Jean and myself. Morrison was trained as a violinist, but this career was disrupted when two members of his family died in quick succession. They had been running the family building business, known as "Morrison Dunbar", and since Morrison was the sole member of the family who could carry it on, it was a case of goodbye to fiddling and getting to grips with the practicalities of trade. Violin playing however was in his bones and he has never lost his love of the fiddle and interest in music. He had a contract with the BBC in Glasgow, to refurbish the building, offices and studios as required, so it was easy for him to pop in and see me whenever he was there to oversee his workmen, and he was a keen supporter of our studio concerts and all our public events.

With Morrison, Jean and I played through just about all the available trio sonatas for two violins and piano. A marvellous sight reader, he produced a very refined, sweet sound from his violin, and what a violin it was—the Alard Stradivarius violin of 1715! How I envied him!. We eventually became neighbours, for when Jean and I bought two acres of land at Lochgoilhead, the vendor said, "If you want privacy, the adjacent acres are for sale—have you a friend who might buy them?". Had I a friend!? Morrison took one look at the two acres and immediately bought it, and so our friendship flourished. He sponsored the Master Series of recitals in Glasgow and together with a colleague, presented a prize for sonata playing at the Royal Scottish Academy of Music and Drama, which I adjudicated on several occasions. On my retirement from the BBC, Morrison and I formed a quartet and we played through all the Haydn and Beethoven quartets. After all the years of hard slog, to just play for the sheer enjoyment of it was great fun.

Morrisons fondness for music did not prevent him from running his business and rose to the top of his profession when he was appointed president of the Builders Association of Great Britain. He was also honoured by becoming a director of the St Mary's School for Young Musicians in Edinburgh as well as a director of the Royal Scottish Academy of Music.

Since our venture of buying a piece of land in Lochgoilhead had mopped up all my spare cash, we had to postpone building a bungalow and made do with a huge caravan fastened to the ground to which we had electricity and running water laid on, water like wine, straight from a mountain stream. The caravan was beautifully equipped with sitting room with a cosy stove, double bedroom, galley and bathroom with a hip bath and pull lavatory. We turned up the wireless when anyone entered the latter compartment. As a weekend retreat it was ideal. Apart from being intimate, we could clean it up in half an hour.

Our cat had a great time hunting, unaccustomed as he was to the country, but we drew the line one morning when he arrived home and deposited a mouse on our pillow. He was a Siamese, very fierce with his own kind but gentle to the point of sloppiness with us. We couldn't think of a name for him until I remembered a pupil of mine from Singapore, Kee Yong, and so it was settled.

During the summer we enjoyed this rural life, in spite of being attacked most viciously by the midges which nearly drove us crazy. By four in the afternoon we had to retire from our duties in the garden and close all the windows.

Family portrait, 1916
and below:
My grandfather's row of houses in Montrose

Four Generations:
Sebastian, on my lap, my parents, and my mother's mother, seated.

Sebastian

Rupert-Oliver

Above:
The Aeolian Quartet
in 1946
Alfred Cave,
Leonard Dight
Watson Forbes
John Moore

Below:
Sir Edward Elgar,
shortly before his death,
looking at the Aeolian
Quartet's recording of his
Piano Quintet. This was the
last piece of music he
listened to before he died.

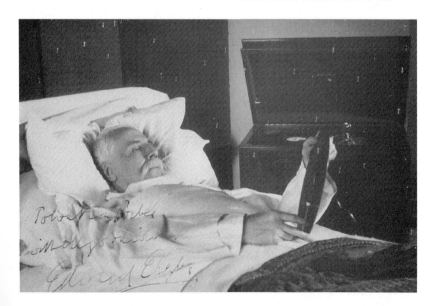

The London String Trio:
with Maria Lidka & Vivian Joseph

With Denise Lassimone

Above:
The Aeolian Quartet in 1960 with
Sydney Humphreys, Trevor Williams
and Derek Simpson

Below:
The London Piano Quartet with
Manny Hurwitz, Vivian Joseph
and Edith Vogel

The great viola player
William Primrose

Two Old Fiddlers: with John Moore in 1991

The Aeolian Quartet in 1953,
with Sydney Humphreys, Colin Sauer and John Moore

Alan Richardson

Jimmy Gibb

Conducting at Downe House
Summer School

Jean, my wife.

View of Loch Ghoil

Despite this, the setting was one of the loveliest in Scotland.

Alas, in January 1968, our dream world was shattered. A terrible storm raged wildly that never to be forgotten night (winds of 90 to 100 mph.). Fortunately none of us were in the caravan, which was completely destroyed, and most of which we could see on the bed of the loch. Meanwhile, in Glasgow, doors banged, windows rattled, roofs were ripped apart—the next morning poor old Glasgow looked like a bombed city. And it was during the morning that a friend rang to tell us we hadn't got a caravan any more. Some of the structure had wrapped itself around the electricity pole and kept on shorting–out the electricity supply to the village!

After this disaster we had to think very quickly what to do, and decided to build a bungalow. I had great fun designing our new home of wood, with large picture windows right down to the ground. Armed with the insurance money we received for the loss of our caravan, and nothing daunted, I found a builder who would erect my design for our limited means. There were only very slight alterations from my plan; it was up in no time and by the summer we were happily ensconced in our bungalow, called Aeolian Cottage for obvious reasons, which Jean adored and where we spent the next ten years. During these happy years we succeeded in making a lovely garden under the most adverse circumstances, for the ground had to be drained and the reeds grew like white fangs in a stubborn mouth, absolute terrors to uproot. We really did work like navvies and had our reward, for we planted literally hundreds of daffodils, many roses, azaleas and rhododendrons, so that people passing in the road used to stop and stare! In fact, one day, one of the villagers stopped me and said, "I must congratulate you"—I preened myself and thought he was congratulating me on the recent award of a Doctorate of Music conferred on me by Glasgow University. I was on the point of saying, "That's all right, just call me Watson" when he anticipated my remark by saying, "Your garden looks magnificent". Humbly, I thanked him and had to confess that the garden was largely the work of my wife.

I was approaching sixty–three when I retired from the BBC. I had had enough of a desk job by that time, administration had its rewards but they were limited. Power and position had almost gone to my head—but not quite! I

97

had stuck to my ideas and they had worked out well, though the strain had been demanding and such success as had been achieved had been won through dedication and hard slog. In fact, I was exhausted. The BBC Scottish Symphony Orchestra had survived, though its future was still precarious. The Radio Orchestra had won through, but was disbanded shortly after I left. A history of Scottish music had been written at my instigation, and a series of records of Scottish music was also in evidence. Folk music, dance and pipe music were all in a flourishing state, as well as composers and performers who were well to the fore in broadcast music.

We had established a close liaison with the then Professor of Music at Glasgow University, Frederick Rimmer (who had succeeded Robin Orr), where the music archive seemed to be well established. We had a close ties with the Royal Scottish Academy of Music and Drama, and often gave their most promising students a pathway into the profession. Our backing of Scottish Opera had produced rewarding results—soon to be frittered away through poor administration—but our relationship with the Edinburgh Festival was on a sure footing, as also were our annual appearances at the London Proms. All in all it was a success story, and one which contributed greatly to the awakening of music in Scotland.

I retired from the active scene and we sold the Glasgow house, electing to live at Lochgoilhead. A complete rest was needed just then, and time to take stock and plan a new life in music—quite different from anything that had gone before.

Free from the hurly–burly of the BBC, life had to be re–planned. My one overwhelming desire was to have a break—a year's sabbatical. To enter the music profession again as a player (and have people say "poor old Forbes, he used to be quite a player") was just not on, and neither were teaching nor administration. I had done all that and I've never found repetition attractive. Gradually though, the interest in making arrangements for the meagre viola repertoire reared its head once again and I began also to make collections of pieces for different instruments for educational purposes, some of these in collaboration with Alan Frank at OUP. I began again to adjudicate and examine for the Associated Board and so before the year was out, the problem of occupation had been solved and these activities kept me happy and occupied for the next fifteen years. Now, also, there was time to play the viola, and the violin, again, but only for 'home consumption', and Jean and I have given many evenings of music and poetry to our long suffering friends.

I had often heard about musicians being captured and interned and becoming the focal point of entertainment in prisoner of war camps, how they had written plays, composed music and generally become the moving spirit in the business of whiling away the weary hours of captivity. I envied their accomplishments and imagined that such things were beyond my limited powers, but gradually Jean and I realised that our neighbours were expecting us to start doing something, and eventually we became the focal point of their expectations. So, nothing daunted, we set about organizing something, and in the end we accomplished quite a lot.

We put on a concert in the church of Vivaldi's *The Seasons*, with Sydney Humphreys playing the solo part. Originally, Vivaldi had written sonnets to illustrate in words what he had portrayed in the music so I asked Jean's son, Michael to write some appropriate sonnets. He came back with a sheaf of poems and was not a little put out when I said that sonnets, not poems were what I wanted. Seething with fury he reluctantly set about transposing them into sonnet form and the result is some of the best work he has ever done. Another poet in the village, Ann Murray, also wrote some sonnets in the style of Vivaldi and both sets were read at the performance which was a great success.

For another event, nearer Christmas time, we enacted the story of St Nicholas and formed a small choir of people from the village to sing Bach chorales at appropriate moments. The choir was led by Bessie McLeod, the local postmistress, a woman of uncertain age but with an enchanting quality of voice, very fresh and young, like an untrained Isobel Baillie. Her husband was the only available tenor and he caused me considerable anxiety by informing me he could only read Sol-Fa. It was the devil's own job trying to remember my school day adventures into Sol-Fa, but somehow, with enormous effort and a considerable amount of bad language the transfer was effected and all was well. The *chef d'oeuvre* of the evening was James Gibb and myself singing the bass line!

Many of these events were very taxing to my administrative and arranging capacities, but much more of a trial was when I ventured on composing music to be sung. Jean had taken over from me the task of writing rhyming verse, and I have reluctantly to admit that she is much better at it than I ever succeeded in being. The idea came to write a play with music, with a narrator declaiming rhyming verse to further the plot, which was simple and exploited local folk-lore. As the ruins of Castle Carrick were at the end of the Loch, it was easy to invent a malevolent giant, with dungeons and a jailer, who disliked children. A fair maiden was captured, rescued by her swain, and in the dénouement the giant repented of his wickedness and all lived happily ever after. I wrote a chorus for the children and Jean and I struggled long to teach them to dance—no mean task this! We called this musical masterpiece "The Goilies", and there was an overture, incidental music, a song for the heroine, a patter song for the repentant giant, and we mustn't forget the dance of the seven veils—though she didn't discard enough of them—and all this musical effort by Watson Forbes! Jeans verse was a spectacular success. Staged at the village hall, the audience loved it, booing the giant, clapping in all the wrong places and generally making it a real Wow. We had to repeat it the next night! Fame at last.

Even more ambitious was a production of Burns's Cantata *The Jolly Beggars* which portrays an evening in Pussy Nancy's bar where a diverse assortment of low-life characters assemble to drink away the fleeting hours. Burns's narrator picturesquely knits together the songs of the various characters with verse and Scottish airs. We had the invaluable services of Duncan Robertson to produce and imported three students from the Academy in Glasgow for the principal parts, with villagers for the chorus. The whole cantata was performed in costume in our own music room, with spot lighting and suitable music arranged for violin and piano. Sally Dunbar made a brilliant narrator and her lovely speaking voice fairly set the tone of the evenings entertainment.

In 1975 I was invited to adjudicate at a music festival in

Hong Kong. I accepted the invitation with alacrity and took Jean along with me since it was to be our first adventure outside Europe. We were most hospitably received, and from our hotel in Kowloon were quite overwhelmed by our first view of the harbour at night. For the music classes we crossed by ferry to Hong Kong from the mainland, and were very impressed by the orderliness and cleanliness of the Chinese. One stood shoulder to shoulder but there was no hustling or jostling either on arrival or boarding—far in advance of our own public transport.

They worked me hard, nine till five every day with an occasional evening session as well. There were huge classes to adjudicate, often of a very high standard, mostly pianists. It was fortunate that the piano repertoire was fairly familiar, so that I was rarely caught napping. Jean had mapped out extensive sight seeing tours for herself while I toiled away but she cancelled nearly all of them for the standard of performance was so exalted and fascinating that she came to every session. Seated at my table was an assistant who translated my remarks from the platform. It was fun hearing these, though it was a little disconcerting to crack a joke and have to wait until it was translated to enjoy the hoped for laughter. It pleased the authorities no end to find that their time–table was strictly adhered to and the results of each class promptly announced. We had a crowded audience most of the time and struck up a friendly relationship with these enthusiastic people. I was told that there were more pianos per square mile in Hong Kong than anywhere else in the world—and I could well believe it. Sundays were free from classes and the ensuing rest was a real boon.

I had been told before leaving England that I must get in touch with a Chinese man who owned several Stradivarius instruments; and duly telephoned his number hoping to make contact. Alas, I had the shortest telephone call I'd ever experienced. 'May I speak to Mr L, please?' 'No' was the curt answer and down went the phone at the other end! I discussed this with my girl assistant, my amanuensis, who undertook to make an appointment for us, which she managed somehow to do. What had we expected? In keeping with a collection of Stradivarius instruments we had every justification in expecting to meet an aristocratic gentleman of some obvious substance. Jean, of course, letting her imagination run away with her, was sure that we would meet an elderly Chinese Mandarin in beautiful silken robes and a houseful of exquisite china and ivory! Imagine our surprise, therefore, when confronted by a man in leather jacket, looking as though he had just arrived on a motor bike. We were presently joined by his wife and transported to an unambitious cafe. We had heard so much about the excellence of real Chinese cooking that we were a little taken aback at the meagre portions and the uninteresting content. However, the couple were charming and we were eventually taken to their flat—a modest dwelling (not a Chinese carpet in sight!) and only then did the evening come alive. Now, all this time our host had been addressing me as Watson Forbes's son and no amount of saying my name and pointing to myself would persuade him that indeed I *was* Watson Forbes! It was not until the end of the evening after about three hours, when he produced my arrangement of a Handel Sonata, and was delighted when we offered to play it for him that, for some unknown reason, the penny dropped and it dawned upon him that perhaps I really was the Watson Forbes that he was talking about, and not his son! Such is fame!

We eventually departed after an evening such as I had never previously experienced; such an array of splendid violins and violas by famous Cremonese makers. I was told afterwards that he also owned some distinguished cellos, including a Strad. He was obviously a successful business man who had invested his money in instruments. Houses had risen in value, whilst Stradivarius instruments were still modestly priced. Since then, fiddles have shot up to command astronomical sums, so he must be an exceedingly rich man by any standards!

We were fascinated by the shops and spent most of our free time window shopping, and buying some of the many coloured materials. Needless to say I had shirts made by 'Sam' the tailor who, to my astonishment, without any deposit or payment of any sort, allowed me to take them back to the hotel to try them on, saying, "If they don't fit bring them back and we'll alter them". They fitted, and I did go back and pay for them! Jean had the same experience, things made most beautifully and expertly for her. She had brought with her an evening blouse for which she wanted to find some material for a skirt to go with it. The Thai girls in the shop were very intrigued and wanted to know where she had bought the blouse. On saying 'Glasgow', they asked where it was made. Well, in the end we looked at the label and you can guess the answer, Hong Kong! The whole shop was in fits of laughter as only the Chinese can laugh.

Some friends, the Boydells, were going on to Bangkok and tried to persuade us to accompany them, but sadly I had just heard of my father's death, so it was imperative to return home to my mother who was on her own.

From the age of fifty–five till sixty–eight we lived in Scotland. It was an interesting experience. We were given a warm welcome and made several good friends during our stay—though I was often treated as one who had strayed away from home and had at last seen the light and returned to my native land! The Scots give only grudging acknowledgement to their poets, painters and musicians. They tend to cling to their haggis, tartan and bagpipes, despite the energy devoted by some of their compatriots to get away from this image. I think the Scots would prefer to look after their own affairs more than is possible at present. Some form of devolution seems desirable.

For the last year of our stay in Lochgoilhead we were approached by the Workers' Educational Association to give six illustrated talks on music, which we agreed to do in our own music room. These were a great success, the village folk supported us splendidly, coming through fog, rain, snow and storm to attend our talks. We covered such topics as the string quartet, opera, Scottish traditional music and song—always with recorded or live illustrations. Later we had the satisfaction of learning that of all the courses the WEA ran, ours was the best attended.

We finally decided to leave Lochgoilhead with great regret, especially from Jean who never seemed to get tired of the place. We had made many friends including the proprietor of the only restaurant, the Bouquet Garni, and it was here we decided to spend our last evening having a jolly good meal. So, as it was a very small restaurant, we rang up and booked a table in advance. On the night, we arrived early and had the place to ourselves. Gradually, however, it began to fill with many of the locals and a surprising number of our dear friends. Slowly it dawned on us that this was no coincidence, a fact confirmed when Bessie (from the Post Office) got up and made a wonderful speech. Jean was nearly in tears. The evening ended with many songs, Bessie singing and Jean playing the piano. What a touching send–off it was.

Why did we leave Scotland, especially Loch Goil? It had so much to recommend it. The mountains were marvellous! The view over the loch, which was studded with little boats and one beautiful schooner, was spectacular. The bungalow (built to my own design) was everything we wanted and we had two acres of ground. It was a truly romantic spot. Rowing across the loch for food was great fun on a good day, and otherwise we had a small local shop within walking distance. It did rain a great deal, and in the summer there were millions of midges, but on the other hand, thanks to the Gulf Stream which flows up the west coast of Scotland, the weather was often mild. Sadly, what had been a paradise was slowly being whittled away as a developer got busy, and chalets and caravans proliferated over the hills. The road which had been practically deserted became a highway and then Argyll was expanded into Strathclyde and the rates leapt up in order to subsidise the indiscretions of Glasgow. But chiefly we left to be nearer our families who had gradually congregated around London.

We decided to move South again. Where to? That was the vital question. We had often remarked that Warwickshire was a seemingly unspoiled county and Jean had spent some years of her youth in Stratford–upon–Avon. So we explored the countryside between Stratford and Oxford, finding many lovely Cotswold villages just off the beaten track. Finally we settled on a house in Great Wolford, a village about fifteen miles south of Stratford with 150 inhabitants and about 250 cows. (Sometimes the cows are preferable to the populace). Our first visit to Wolford was scarcely auspicious. I have for some reason a great antipathy to church bells and we arrived as wedding bells were clanging maddeningly. Also, wafting towards us from the gate of the farm opposite was the most pungent odour of silage. Bravely ignoring these perils we marched in to the house to find it had everything we were looking for; a large studio for our music room and a truly beautiful garden. We have lived here happily ever since.

We were very fortunate in finding on our arrival in Great Wolford an enthusiastic, enlightened and tolerant vicar, the Reverend Woodward Court, who was delighted to welcome us to his church and encouraged us to put on our various shows, musical and theatrical, in the church. In a performance of Vivaldi's Seasons, Jean read her son's rendering of the composer's sonnets, with myself as solo violinist, and a piano quintet. On another occasion we were lucky to find an excellent singer in Caroline McCausland to sing some of my brother–in–law George Beckwith's songs, which she enjoyed so much that she included some of them in her Queen Elizabeth Hall recitals. George, who had written much music for the famous Maddermarket Theatre in Norwich, also provided us with a dramatisation of the Book of Job and an Everyman Nativity Play. In this last, the children were delighted by the live donkey walking up the aisle. (I would like to add that it behaved immaculately)

Then, Bernard and Sylvia Knight, former viola players in the Scottish National Orchestra and now neighbours of ours living in a village very near to Great Wolford, founded The Cotswold Sinfonietta. The orchestra consists entirely of highly–skilled professional players resident in the Midlands. I was invited to become the orchestra's President and was often consulted on musical matters and introduced many of the orchestra's programmes.

To avoid repeating ourselves as a viola and piano duo, I have continued to raid the violin and cello repertoire, and duly arranged sonatas by Bach, Handel, Beethoven, Brahms, Cesar Franck, Mendelssohn and Dvorák for the viola. These sounded very acceptable and kept me busily occupied scribbling away. After a performance of Beethovens Spring Sonata, one of our audience remarked, "That sonata is also arranged for the violin isn't it?".

While I was working in Scotland, I made many friends at the Royal Scottish Academy of Music and Drama. It was most gratifying, in 1983, to be invited on three successive years to be the external examiner for the end of year string examinations. This I enjoyed enormously and the whole week was very friendly and relaxed, though hard work. Very pleasant relationships were formed with the Principal, Philip Ledger, the Head of the String Department, Peter Mountain and James Durrant, senior viola teacher. In 1987 I was elected a Fellow of the RSAMD for distinguished services to music. Having already, some years previously, received an Honorary Doctorate from the University of Glasgow, I feel that Scotland has indeed done me proud.

The occasion of conferring the Fellowship at the Royal Academy of Music and Drama in Scotland was very festive. It took place in the morning—in the forenoon as we say in Scotland—as part of the annual prize–giving ceremony for the students of the Academy who have distinguished themselves during the academic year. There were four new Fellows elected: Cicely Berry, the distinguished voice director to the Royal Shakespeare Company, Alex McCrindle, the well known stage, TV, radio and film actor, Peter Mountain, and my humble self. My son, Rupert Oliver, with his wife Elisabeth and my grandson Bruce, who did full justice to the refreshment table, arrived from Switzerland, and my stepson Michael, had flown in from Saudi Arabia for the event. So, together with the support of many old friends from Glasgow and Edinburgh, I felt doubly honoured. The evening was given over to a huge dinner party and as I had to deliver a brief speech *after* dinner I spent the meal looking longingly at my overflowing glasses of wine. Altogether a memorable and most enjoyable day. It was, in fact, the last event to be held in the old building. The Academy moved into their new building in the following autumn.

After retiring from examining and adjudicating, I found I had no definite commitments during the winter months. For the first time in my life there was freedom to come and go—I chose to go! So, after much discussion, we decided to try spending the winter months in the South of Spain, enjoying the sunshine of Sotogrande, about ten miles east of Gibraltar, instead of the rigours of the English climate, from December to March in 1984, 1985 and 1986. Needless to say, idleness was not the order of the day! Failing to find a piano in this part of Spain, we decided on an electronic keyboard which fitted nicely into the back seat of the car. Jean hates it and wants to kick it every time she sees it, but it serves its purpose and keeps her fingers moving and allows us to play together, (and anyway she threatened me with instant divorce if she had to listen to unaccompanied Bach or indeed any form of unaccompanied viola for four months on end). We use it to give three concerts of music and verse each year at the local hotel, no-one complains, and it is a great joy for Jean when we reach home and she can at last sit down again at her heavenly Blüthner.

The trips to Spain for the winter months were a great success. We rented a very commodious flat (so there was room for our sons and their ever increasing families). There was a minute garden with a lovely patio where we could have our drinks and lunch, with a view of the Mediterranean in the distance. We overlooked a copse of eucalyptus and cork trees, with a beautiful old white building—an ancient monastery, now the international school—about a mile away as the crow flies. What really endeared us to this particular spot was the unbelievable peace and quiet. One could wander in the cork woods behind our flat hearing only the sound of birds and the occasional neigh of a horse in the distance—not even the noise of a petrol engine. Slowly, too, as January turned into February, a multitude of wild flowers would begin to appear. Whatever one's mood, there one could walk and come back refreshed and ready to carry on with whatever job one had on hand.

Chapter 11

Hobbies

Of course, being born in St Andrews, I should have been a keen golfer, but somehow I never took to the game. I did play, but only under duress, and soon abandoned the sport. I preferred walking without the hazard of losing a ball, or my temper, every half mile. I have always been fond of wine, reading about it, drinking it and making it, and on confessing to my hobbies for 'Who's Who in Music' I wrote 'Wine'. In recent years I have enjoyed making sherry and vermouth from tins of essence; sadly the days of making wine from fresh fruit are over—too much trouble! I have sampled wines from many countries but never become proficient in detecting from nose and taste which wine is which—I just enjoy the wine for what it is. It may sound as if I am an addict or an alcoholic, but in fact my ration is at most two glasses of sherry before lunch, two glasses of wine in the evening, plus an occasional whisky to please my wife, who declares that whisky is good for the elderly.

I have always been fond of cruising on the English canals, such a fine, quiet, relaxing affair. At four miles per hour, flat out, one has time to see the world, contemplate nature and laugh at the folly of sheer speed. One bank holiday, cruising at our usual andante tempo, we were able to view with a certain smug satisfaction a traffic jam on the M1 with which the canal ran parallel. However, the trouble with motor cruisers, whether owned or hired, is the quixotic behaviour of engines. On one occasion we felt the ignominy of being towed home—by a canoe! Another time the engine suddenly packed up when a huge tug was bearing down on us. I waved my handkerchief frantically and finally got it to 'heave to'. As it stopped, almost broadside on across the canal, our engine suddenly sprang into life and, albeit slightly out of control, the brilliant navigation of 'Captain' Watson Forbes enabled us to slip through the rapidly closing gap left between the tug and the bank. Looking back we saw that the tug was well and truly stuck from bank to bank. We felt faintly ashamed, but triumphant. My grandfather would have been proud of me!

I had often scanned the advertisements for a dream voyage on a heavenly sea, lying on the deck in glorious sunshine with some glamorous beauty attending to my every want! Such a dream actually came true, when our friend Ian Meikle asked us to come to Greece and tour the islands on a hired caique. We flew to Athens, paid our respects to the Acropolis, watched a *son et lumiere* display, and finally went to Piraeus to join the boat. It seemed small to accommodate a crew of two, Jean's son Philip, as well as Ian and the pair of us. However, once aboard there was ample room.

In blissful, sunny weather we sailed around the islands landing each evening for a sumptuous meal—rather fun, since one was usually welcome to invade the kitchen to see what was cooking, and choose one's own 'bit'. One morning when our early morning cup of tea arrived, we discovered we were moored at an uninhabited island where we could take a flying leap into the glorious, translucent water. We visited Hydra, the Corinth Canal and other beautiful and historic places. One of the highlights of the holiday was a performance of Agamemnon by Aeschylus, given in the huge open–air theatre at Epiderus. It was a marvellous experience and one on which we dwelt for many a day.

It was a great joy for me to take over the wheel from the captain and steer the boat. I felt like a small boy being given a surprise treat—it made me feel very important! Particularly enchanting was the experience of being at the wheel during a journey after dark, there was something so romantic about the distant lights and the motion of the boat. So, too, was the evening when we visited the island where the captain and his mate had their respective homes. First we were entertained in the mate's house and given some strange home–made liqueur, from whence we proceeded to the captain's house where we were again given most generous hospitality. Finally we ended up in the only restaurant on the small island, where a special meal and good fellowship were the order of the evening. In fact the whole fortnight was a delight and something we shall never forget; a dream come true.

As a teacher and performer I had often thought about viola construction, size and set–up but, not surprisingly, had made no attempt to build one. For a start I had no experience in woodwork, and the use of saws, knives and gouges was not a practice to be recommended for a string player. However, when I reached the age of 82, Jean suggested that this was something I could attempt. My friend, Rex England, had given talk at a musical evening at our home sometime before, so I had a very general idea of the processes involved. I contacted Rex again and told him of my ideas, and if he was somewhat taken aback he concealed it well. He later confided that he felt it was rather as if he himself, a very limited viola player, had decided to tackle the Walton Concerto.

He came to see me armed with an internal mould of an Amati brothers copy, assuring me that this was probably the easiest method to employ. As I had only a few tools at that time he also brought a set of ribs that he had already bent to shape, and the neck and corner blocks. A set of written instructions and recommendations on where to obtain tools books, maple and spruce were sufficient to enable me to make a start. My family were extremely supportive and the summer house was converted to a workshop with a bench and the basic tools. I had to learn as I went along with the help of other makers, and friends and family with wood-working experience. I had to learn that wood is a very variable material and has to be worked carefully, taking into account its grain and structure. I had to learn how to use the traditional violin makers' glue and had to attempt the difficult techniques involved with purfling and the thicknessing of plates. The scroll presented problems of accurate carving, and patience and perseverance were the qualities most required.

After about a year, and hundreds of hours of work, the viola was varnished and set up. Like many first attempts it is much too heavy. I have named it 'The Bass Rock' after the massive granite outcrop in the Firth of Forth. The name reflects not so much the quality of the lower strings but rather, as Rex England observed, its general appearance of rugged grandeur and Scottish indestructibility. Did I enjoy making it? I have already started on Viola No. 2!

We still enjoy gardening. My wife and I share the work— she does the planting, weeding, picking the flowers, pruning the roses and generally tidying up. I do the heavy stuff, mow the lawn, see to the compost heap, dig holes for new plants and oversee the buying of shrubs and rose trees. Compared with other gardens around, ours is a bit untidy, but we honestly don't like things planted in straight immaculate rows. Ours is a wild garden, and what it fails to achieve in orderliness it more than makes up for in vigour of growth and colour. We even have time, occasionally, to sit and admire our handiwork. In the autumn we tidy up as best we can, plant as many bulbs as possible and then leave the garden to mature, or whatever it does during the dreary months of winter. In the spring the whole cycle of activity starts afresh.

Chapter 12

Coda

Some months before my seventy–fifth birthday, unbeknown to me, my wife Jean was trying to arrange a celebration for that event, greatly assisted by Bernard Knight and John White, (a former pupil and now Professor of Viola at the Royal Academy) and gloriously she achieved her aim. Secretly, she wrote postcards to many of my older colleagues and friends, saying, *"Can you come to a celebration on such and such a date, etc., please don't answer—when I get the opportunity I will ring you up and find out if you can come—for I want it to be a complete surprise for Watson"*. It certainly worked. She told me afterwards that her first idea had been to ask the Academy if they would let us have a room for pre-lunch drinks. To her fury, the request was turned down, on the excuse that it might create a precedent. Rescue came from Morrison Dunbar, who, hearing of this set-back, and as a member of the Garrick club, arranged for the proceedings to take place there.

And so it turned out. Sally and Morrison Dunbar invited us to lunch at the Garrick Club as a birthday treat, so all unknowing we arrived for drinks before lunch and then the fun began. As we were quietly having our first sherry, in walked my elder son Sebastian, with his family, followed to my even greater surprise by my younger son, Rupert Oliver and his small boy Bruce, having flown from Switzerland. After which there came a host of friends too numerous to mention, students, former colleagues from the various ensembles to which I had belonged, publishers and musicians with whom I had been associated together with Jean's three sons and their families. My whole life was portrayed before me. We had drinks and refreshments, the *pièce de résistance* being a birthday cake made in the shape of a viola (the seventy–five candles were not forgotten either!). Then Jimmy Gibb made a speech in my honour, and with barely time to collect my thoughts I managed to reply. A true celebration. I was quite overwhelmed by the warmth and affection of the assembly as well as by the numerous presents showered upon me.

This was not the end of the festivities. The following March, John White organised a concert at the Royal Academy of Music in my honour. The afternoon was spent hearing his students play—how jolly well they played—and discussing their various technical and musical problems. In the evening some of my old colleagues played before a distinguished audience in the Duke's Hall. Emmanuel Hurwitz (violin) and Trevor Williams (viola) played Mozart's Duo in G K423, James Gibb performed Schubert's Piano Sonata in A D664 and also gave a moving and eulogistic speech about me. The young Bochmann String Quartet played Mozart's String Quartet in D minor K421 and their viola player Martin Outram with his pianist Deborah Shah gave a very sensitive account of the *Autumn Sketches* by Alan Richardson and our arrangement of the *Six Country Dances* by Beethoven.

For the first time in a long career, as I walked into the hall I was given a standing ovation!

At the beginning of these memoirs I declared that the three loves of my life were wine, woman and string quartets. I have expanded on my love of wine, and dealt in some detail on my love of string quartets and how this gradually transferred itself, as life so often dictates, towards the fiddle. You may say 'What about women?' Well, it may be a natural reticence on my part, or a deep respect for the women in question, but really the case is simpler than either of these half–baked excuses—in other words, to write about women in my life would take a volume in itself. So, I will only say 'Bless them for making life less humdrum' and pass on, if you will excuse me.

I had an odd experience the other day. I had to complete one of those Inland Revenue forms where you have to give your name, age, sex and so on, but I got into rather a quandary when it came to 'Occupation'. I wrote in 'Musician', in pencil in case I changed my mind, and then indeed I did pause and considered all the music that had been written that I knew nothing about at all, and I thought, 'I can't put down Musician', so I erased it and thought again. I tried again with 'Administrator', but I had ceased to be an administrator so I scored *that* out and wrote instead 'Adjudicator', but even this was all wrong, for I have retired from adjudicating. In the end, having pondered deeply, I simply wrote 'Fiddler'! And so I sent off the form, and it was accepted—at least it was not returned. But it's true. A fiddler I have been all my life. I fell in love with the sound of the fiddle when I was about four years old, and I have loved it ever since—the sound of the fiddle, the playing of the fiddle and, indeed, looking back, the whole of my life has been one long... fiddle.

* * *

Appendix I

The Viola and its Repertoire

First Published as Articles in 'The Strad'
Magazine

Although the viola is the oldest member of the violin family, it has been the last to develop a solo repertoire of its own. Once the most important string instrument, it slowly gave way to the violin and 'cello and remained useful solely to fill the gap in pitch between these two instruments. Not a very illustrious position! Part writing in the sixteenth and early seventeenth centuries gave no great individuality to the inside parts and therefore no great demand was made on technique.

In those days it was the viola tenore that was used—a larger and more powerful instrument than the viola alto which only came into general use about the middle of the seventeenth century.

At that period composers sometimes wrote chamber music to include separate parts for both the violas—the higher part being taken by the alto and the lower part, written in the tenor clef, by the viola tenore. Although smaller in tone, the alto was easier to handle and greater technical feats could be accomplished. Whether it was because composers were making greater demands on the inside parts than ever possible on the tenore or, conversely, that the introduction of the alto was providing them with greater scope, this latter instrument had definitely come to stay. It soon superseded the tenore, the extinction of which was only a matter of time. Even so, during the eighteenth and most of the nineteenth centuries anything above the third position on the viola was always hazardous, and it was not till the latter part of the nineteenth and the beginning of the present centuries that the full compass of the viola began to be exploited.

If we consider the violin as the ideal model for a string instrument, the viola must be classed as a compromise. From a structural point of view the body is too small for the pitch of the strings. This is unavoidable. To hold and play the viola like a cello has been found impracticable; since therefore the viola must be held in a similar way to the violin, the length and depth of the body must be governed by the length of the average human arm and neck. The result of this anomaly is that the tone differs considerably from the violin; it is in fact less brilliant, being slightly muffled and in some models rather nasal, but capable of a warm and sympathetic tone on its lower strings and considerable penetrating power in the upper register. Early composers were content to treat it as an inner part in the string ensemble roughly corresponding to the tenor voice in the vocal quartet. But slowly a change took place, the very defects of the viola becoming its greatest asset. Composers became aware of its distinctive tone-colour and its originality as a solo instrument in quartet and orchestra. Modern composers have taken this one step further by writing for it solos, sonatas and concertos.

One of the chief drawbacks to the viola asserting itself as a solo instrument on its own merits has been that in many ways its technique is similar to that of the violin. Add to this the fact that in most of the concerted music of the eighteenth and early nineteenth centuries the viola part is considerably easier than the first violin and often not so 'exposed' as the second violin and there is ample encouragement for disappointed violin players changing to the viola. It might even seem that at one time this was the only way new recruits were found. The standard of playing was very poor in consequence and must have resulted in a deadlock in which on the one side composers would not write interesting music for bad players, and on the other, no good violin player would take to the viola to play the dull parts composers provided. What the viola really lacked was a performer–composer or a player enthusiastic and brilliant enough to influence composers to write worthwhile music for the instrument.

If we glance at the history of string playing before 1900

we realise that the viola can boast of no illustrious exponents like the violin or cello. Names like Corelli, Paganini, Wieniawski, Spohr, Joachim or again, Goltermann, Popper and Piatti, bear testimony both to the players' skill and the recognised soloistic powers of their respective instruments. Let us consider for a moment the effect these players have had on the repertoire of their instrument and we can see how very handicapped the viola must have been.

The twentieth century, however, has already produced several players illustrious enough to influence the repertoire. Paul Hindemith has so far been the most notable performer who is also celebrated as a composer for his instrument; but others, by their influence and collaboration have persuaded composers to write music for them with equally successful results. I think we may safely boast that the viola players of this country represented by Lionel Tertis, William Primrose, Bernard Shore and followed by a host of enthusiastic younger players have been the pioneers of this movement, and have already been responsible for the introduction of many masterpieces, thereby changing the whole aspect of the viola repertoire. So important have many of these proved to be that the position of the viola as a solo instrument is now assured.

When we take into account the size of the viola we can realise that it is well beyond the reach and strength of young students till they reach the age of sixteen to eighteen, so that even today most, though not all, viola players have had their earliest training as violinists. This certainly explains the great shortage of teaching material for the early stages of technical development and the makeshift policy of 'making do' with transposed violin tutors and first–year pieces.

What makes a violinist decide to become a viola player? Certainly not inability on the violin—the modern viola repertoire takes care of that. It seems it is becoming more usual for violin students to take viola as a second study for at least one term, then temperament or physique combined with an unexpected demand on his services (viola students are usually scarce and over worked), play their part and a new convert is made. The practice of playing both violin and viola is one that is useful among amateurs and where possible a paying proposition amongst professionals, but the modern tendency is to make the viola a full–time study and this is really the most satisfactory way.

One of the greatest problems facing the student of the viola is the question of repertoire. From the foregoing brief sketch it will be evident that most of the solo music has only just been composed and that each new addition is still an event. What does exist, apart from one or two classics, is still too recent to have become well known. But there is a repertoire, and it will be my purpose in the succeeding articles to review exactly what is available, pointing out the various merits of the works mentioned, their relative difficulty and their suitability for professional, student or amateur.

(Reprinted from the Strad Magazine, October 1939)

Tutors, Studies and First Year Pieces

Probably no parent, dreaming of future fame and fortune for his child, will select for him such an instrument so lacking in glamour as the viola. There are no famous violists of the past to stimulate his imagination or encourage the ambitions of the child. It is much more probable that the very pressing requirements of the school orchestra persuades the youngster into having a sporting shot at it—especially as a teacher who can undertake classes in string instruments is usually at hand. Whatever the age of the pupil, the first year's training is the most vital, since he acquires set habits during this time likely to affect the whole of his subsequent career. It is therefore to his lasting advantage, if possible, to commence with a teacher specialising in the viola. It might, however, be stated now, that many specialists find the early stages of training and the sometimes rather unnerving sounds produced by a beginner on a string instrument such as the viola, so tedious, that they prefer to accept the same pupil some years later when he has acquired a technique, adequate, but perhaps faulty in some respects.

Assuming that the instrument of his choice is the viola and the teacher already chosen, the next problem of paramount importance lies with the teacher: 'Which tutor shall I give my pupil?' As the tutor will be the student's first volume of music and probably his sole companion during the first few months of his tuition, it is a choice to which the teacher would do well to give some thought.

It might be assumed that in no department of the repertoire would the viola be so lacking as in tutors and in first year pieces for beginners, yet on examining the case this view will need modifying. Admittedly the demand is small since only a very few viola players really have their early training on the viola, the majority, especially young students, acquiring their initial instruction and early development as violinists. Another condition that might adversely affect the demand is the undoubted fact that viola teachers who deal with beginners are usually both violin and viola players and teachers, and although there may be more demand on their services as viola players, it is certainly true that it is the violin pupils who occupy most of their teaching time. The tendency on the teacher's part may therefore be to make the same teaching material do for both violin and viola pupils whenever possible. On reviewing the tutors and studies thus produced—having the dual purpose of being written for the violin and arranged for the viola a fifth lower—we cannot quarrel with the results. Indeed there is almost complete similarity in the beginning stages of both instruments, the nicer details of technique and tone only occupying the attention of the student at a later stage. Any small difference not covered by the text can easily be explained and demonstrated by the teacher during the lesson. What this amounts to is that all that can be said in favour of the classical violin tutors and studies can be repeated in terms of their viola equivalent.

One of the most popular violin tutors arranged for the viola is that by Berthold Tours. It gives complete instruction from the very beginning and is well illustrated by drawings and photographs of the correct method of holding the viola and bow. It has the advantage of taking the student through the initial difficulties by easy steps and is therefore especially suitable for children. The edition I use is edited by Alfred Gibson but I understand that Novello have a new edition 'in the press' prepared by Bernard Shore. Another tutor presenting the difficulties in a methodical way is the volume by Langey. This book prefaces the practical part with some helpful discussion on the rudiments of music. The exercises and studies are arranged in such easy progressive stages that no pupil can have any difficulty in understanding them, while the short pieces have accompaniments to be played by the teacher as second viola—a very useful addition which will greatly stimulate the pupil's musical outlook. All the celebrated studies, études and caprices used by violin teachers throughout the world are also published in transposed versions for the viola. It is only necessary for me to mention names like Kayser, Mazas, Kreutzer, Rode, Dont, Schradieck, Rovelli and Campagnoli for any teacher to realise that it would be possible to train a viola student from the very commencement up to the higher demands of viola technique without once having to resort to any but violin studies.

There are, however, several viola methods and studies written solely for that instrument. From those which may be ranked as classics I should like to mention Bruni's Viola School which is probably the most celebrated and also the method by Kayser. It should he noted that Bruni's Tutor covers the first stages rather quickly and indeed almost pre–supposes some preliminary instruction from other text books or a slight knowledge of the violin. It does, nevertheless, contain a number of very fine studies. Of those tutors written during the present century I should specially like to include Wesseley's Practical Viola School. This presents the first lessons in the easiest possible way and deals exceptionally well with bowing. There are however, no illustrations or photographs as in the Tutor by Tours, and it is therefore less suitable for younger students. In conjunction with this tutor the same publishers, Joseph Williams, recommend several additional pieces which may well prove useful. There are four by T.F. Dunhill, *In Courtly Company, Alla Sarabande, The Willow Brook*, and *Meditation;* also four slightly harder ones by Alec Rowley, *Aubade, Scherzo, Reverie* and *Farandole*. There are numerous other tutors the teacher might care to examine—by Laubach, Klingenfeld (Viola School for Violinists), Sitt, etc. Among the more recent composers is Adam Carse, who by his writing for the elementary stages of tuition for other instruments has demonstrated that he understands the requirements of the beginner so well. He has published books of Preliminary Exercises and Progressive Studies to form a viola school. Book V of this series has only just been issued. As a new school of viola playing is slowly developing it seems possible that these tutors and studies specially written for the viola will tend more and more to become the standard works.

Most tutors aim at giving complete instruction with studies and pieces included with the text and exercises. It is however, usually advisable to supplement these by separate books of studies and pieces, especially after the early stages have been successfully mastered. If the tutor is entirely written by one composer, this affords relief from the same musical idiom, and if the author introduces a selection from other composers it is rare that he covers all the special requirements of the pupil. Besides, there is the psychological factor to be considered. Nothing is so boring to the pupil than to have to work wearily on through the same book term after term, while on the other hand nothing gives such a stimulus to his enthusiasm than a new book—something fresh to tackle—which gives him a feeling of making progress. In addition to the list of violin studies already mentioned, notable original books of technique have been contributed by Bruni, *Twenty-Five Studies*; Hermann, *The Study of the Viola* and *Concert Studies*; and Kreuz, *Progressive Studies* (complete with a second viola part). Advanced players can find additional material in the *Orchestral Studies* of Wagner and Strauss.

Over and above all these books of studies, there have become available in recent years various selections from the above mentioned works, chosen and grouped for special purposes and usually arranged in order of difficulty. These anthologies of the classics vary greatly in their selection but most of them can be recommended, the ultimate choice being guided as much by the inclusion of a particular teacher's favourite study rather than any great superior merit of one volume over another. Three books of Viola Technique by Steiner comprise selections from Bruni, Hoffmeister, Campagnoli, etc., and five books of Studies, arranged by Kreuz can also be recommended. Most of the classical violin pieces and arrangements for beginners are available in albums, and in their transposed versions, adapted to the viola, they are just as invaluable. Nearly every publisher has one or more different albums of Celebrated Pieces, Album Leaves, School of Melody, etc., and the teacher who can safely experiment with these various volumes need never get stale through lack of fresh teaching material.

While none of the groups of tutors, studies and pieces mentioned are intended as a complete survey of all the possibilities, I have included those most generally in use and only those which I myself have used or examined. The amount of teaching material published and the amount of thought given to supplying the additional demand created in all branches of music by the increased interest and practice of music in schools is resulting in a greater quantity and an altogether higher standard of music available. The teacher will be well advised to examine some of the more recent additions to pedagogic literature, since many embody a more scientific basis and psychological treatment than the older methods. This is particularly true in music for class teaching and school orchestras and also in children's instruction books. I should like to draw attention to the important and steadily increasing volume of music for beginners in school orchestras, the Polychordia String Library, edited by James Brown deserving special mention, as well as the numerous pieces selected and excellently arranged by Adam Carse and Alec Rowley.

The music that has been reviewed in this article may well cover the first two or three years of the student's musical life and will give him a technique and musical outlook which will prepare him for the study of the pieces and sonatas I will discuss in a later article.

(Reprinted from the Strad Magazine, November 1939)

The Italian Sonata

The word sonata indicates a piece to be sounded, in opposition to cantata—a piece to be sung. Originally any instrumental piece was called a sonata, but during the period from 1625 to 1700 various developments resulted in the sonata becoming a term indicating a collection of various contrasted movements, grouped together by the composer and intended to be played consecutively.

The earliest sonatas, called Sonata da Chiesa, were to be played in a church, while the Sonata da Camera—a secular piece, was for the concert room or 'chamber'. Both forms appeared first in Italy and it was there that those early sonatas chiefly flourished—so much so that we generally refer to instrumental pieces in this form as Italian Sonatas.

The Church Sonata differs from the Chamber Sonata in that the music of the former is strictly abstract while the latter contains numerous movements founded on the dance forms of the day—Gavotte, Minuet, Gigue, etc. The Church Sonata has usually four movements and by its dignity of style and seriousness of purpose may be claimed in many respects as the forerunner of the sonatas of Mozart, Beethoven and Brahms. The movements of the Chamber Sonata vary considerably in number and order, but usually consist of an Allemande, Courante, Sarabande, Gavotte and so on alternately fast and slow finishing with a fast movement, often a Gigue. They are in fact scarcely distinguishable from Suites and Partitas. Most of the later Italian sonatas do not strictly conform to either type and while still alternating slow with fast, have movements which might be difficult to classify as either Church or Secular.

The Italians have one more claim to distinction about this time, for they were the first to make a satisfactory quartet of string instruments. These four, the violin, viola, cello and double bass form the nucleus around which most of the instrumental music from then till the present day has been composed. After years of experimenting with all sorts of violins, viols, violas d'amore, violas da gamba, etc., violin makers slowly approached an ideal, and it was the Amati, the Guarnerius, and the Stradivarius families who finally gave the violin the ideal shape. Whether they actually discovered the perfect size and shape for the viola itself remains open to question.

Again it was an Italian who first showed the joint possibilities of the newly established fiddle and the form of composition known as a sonata. The name of Corelli is one which stands out as being important historically both as a player and composer. He it was who first formed a school of violin playing embodying a firm foundation for all future developments. Though probably limited in his own achievements—he rarely ventured above the third position—the success of his pupils showed the soundness of his principles. As a composer he published about sixty sonatas for varying combinations of instruments, the violin always having the leading part. Although it would be easy to exaggerate his importance as a composer of originality, there is no doubt that he firmly established the Italian sonata form.

As a direct consequence of Corelli's dual role as violinist–composer, the Italian sonata was almost exclusively written for the violin (and to a lesser extent the 'cello) and the developments of violin playing and the Italian sonata form went hand in hand. Thus we have a glorious treasury of violin music from this part of musical history. Corelli's pupils Geminiani and Locatelli further advanced the sonata, and other Italians such as Tartini, Vivaldi, Nardini and Veracini contributed their share. Later, when the idea of the Italian sonata spread to other countries, we find Bach, Handel, Purcell and others writing 'Italian sonatas'.

The viola was decidedly unlucky in those days since no solo sonatas were written for it. If only Corelli had been a viola player! As it is a period which most recitalists like to represent in their programmes, the unfortunate viola player has to rely on arrangements. There is however, every excuse for such arrangements since this style of music probably suffers least in transcription. Occasional exceptions, where the technique is essentially violinistic—as in Tartini's "*Trillo del Diavolo*" are naturally avoided. It is notorious that viola players, through force of circumstance, soon acquire a habit of arranging all kinds of music for their instrument and if they explore this wealth of violin and 'cello literature they will be amply repaid. There are two alternative ways of arranging these sonatas. The first consists of playing the violin part a fifth lower, which means that the same music can be played on a corresponding string with the same fingering. This method overcomes technical difficulties that are truly violinistic, such as the use of an open string in double-stopping, etc. The other method is to keep the sonata in the same key and transfer the solo part to the octave in which it sounds most effective on the viola. This latter method is most favoured by publishers, since the same printed piano part does service for violin and viola, or cello and viola editions.

Of the hundreds of violin and 'cello sonatas, I have been able to trace upwards of thirty arranged and published for the viola. I do not intend to examine in detail all that are available but I should like to deal with a few that have specially interested me.

The Sonata in E minor by Marcello is a particularly happy example It has the usual four movements, is short, and as it rarely goes beyond the third position it may be recommended to those of only average technique. The arrangement by Marchet in Augener's edition is calculated to show off the viola to its greatest advantage by placing the various movements in their best sounding register. Thus the first movement, slow and cantabile, is mainly on the D string; the second, Allegro, is kept fairly high and avoids quick passages on the lower strings which so often sound laboured in this type of music on the viola. There is, however, ample opportunity for C string tone in the third movement, Adagio. The fourth movement is probably the weakest of the sonata but much can be done to make it more interesting by the addition of various bowings—a hint of what I mean may be had from studying the cello part printed above the piano score.

One of the most successful arrangements of a sonata in the Italian style is the Eccles in G minor. An arrangement by Paul Klengel is in the Peters Edition. This is slightly more difficult both musically and technically than the Marcello, the two quick movements, especially the last, demanding a particularly good bowing arm. This sonata, written by an Englishman living in Paris, shows how, by 1720, the musical culture of Italy had spread to other lands. It is fine music

126

both to listen to and to perform.

One of the most difficult of these sonatas arranged for viola is No.3 in D by Leclair (Schott Edition). This composer adds to the Italian mode an element of grace and vivacity peculiarly French. Leclair occupies an important position among classical violinists owing to the new effects in double-stopping he introduced to the violin. Most of the movements of his sonatas have double-stopping and this example is no exception. In consequence this present arrangement is correspondingly more difficult on the viola than on the violin. Whether or not it is wholly successful on the viola in performance, it can nevertheless be recommended as a very good study for advanced players. I should suggest that the second movement be played Allegretto instead of Allegro as marked to give the double-stopping a better chance to sound on the viola. The last two movements, Sarabande and Tambourin, are often played separately from the rest of the sonata and form good examples of Leclair at his very best.

(Reprinted from the Strad Magazine, December 1939)

The Italian Sonata
(continued)

I should like to continue the review by adding to the list some others that have especially interested me and perhaps it would be a good plan to start with the easier sonatas. Here are two that lie well within the average amateur violist's accomplishments and either one might serve as a good introduction to this form of composition for the viola student. They are (1) Sonata No. 3 in G, by Marcello, and (2) Sonata No. 6 in D, by Ariosti.

(1) I have already mentioned a Marcello sonata in E minor, and this present one is similar in many respects. It, too, is short, has four movements, and as the player need never go beyond the third position, it will present no undue difficulty. The music is simple in style and has the characteristic features and charm of the early 18th century violin music—the slow sustained noble melodies, the vigorous allegro with its sequences and 'echo' effects and the 'Poco Scherzando' finale. The arrangement from the

original 'cello part is by Alfred Gibson in Schott's edition. For reference, readers might care to note a printer's error in the omission of the key signature, F sharp, in the third movement, Grave.

The sonata in E minor or the present one in G would be an admirable choice for younger students; Marcello is a useful standby for teachers.

(2) The other easy sonata previously mentioned—that by Ariosti (circa 1660) and called Lezione No. 6a—is one of a set of six in the Schott edition arranged from the original for viola d'amore by Alfredo Piatti. Containing a Corrente, Giga and Rondeaux, it is representative of an earlier period of Italian sonatas when the Church and secular works (Sonata da Chiesa and Sonata da Camera) were still two distinct forms of composition. As this sonata takes the player into the fifth position and also contains some double-stopping, it must be classed as slightly more advanced than the Marcello. Less advanced players who find the double stopping too awkward to be possible in performance, may leave out the lower line in most cases without unduly affecting the music, and I would like to suggest that the first line of the Rondeaux is equally effective, and much easier, played an octave lower.

I have already mentioned how Handel, a German, wrote sonatas in the Italian style. Everyone who knows his excellent set of six violin sonatas will be a little disappointed in the viola da gamba and cembalo sonata that is published for viola and piano. It is called a 'Sonata Concertato' and is the first in this series I have so far discussed where the piano has an equal if not more important part. It is not a solo sonata with piano accompaniment arranged from a figured bass in the traditional style, and in emphasising the duo element foreshadows the later developments of Haydn, Mozart and early Beethoven. Indeed the viola may be said to accompany the piano in many places. It is not quite Handel at his best, with the possible exception of the beautiful and melodious Adagio which forms the third movement. Do not be misled by the look of the three-quaver rhythm in the last movement, it has six crotchets and not four dotted crotchets to the bar! Although it is probably the easiest technically, it is musically the most difficult of the sonatas I have so far analysed in this article and is the therefore less suitable for younger students than the Marcello sonatas. It is published by Augener and edited by Gustav Jensen.

Another useful sonata that teachers might care to note is the Grazioli in F Major. I feel however that the arrangement from the original for cello by Marchet in the Augener edition does not always place the viola part in the happiest register. An arrangement of this essentially simple style of music that consistently lies so high and frequently goes beyond the third position on the A string of the viola seems to introduce a wrong colour and gives a slightly strident sound which is unnatural to the period of the music. This fault is easily overcome by playing some of the passages an octave lower. With this reservation it is a very effective sonata in performance. The criticism, of course, does not apply to the second movement which is calculated to show off the viola to its greatest advantage. It is better to avoid any glissando between the first two notes of the first movement by starting in the second position.

At the beginning of this century it was generally considered that no violin recital programme was complete that did not pay homage to the work of Ferdinand David. He it was who resurrected Bach's solo violin sonatas from oblivion, and who first edited the masterpieces of the 17th and 18th century violinists and made them available to his contemporaries. Without his efforts a rich store of musical culture might still have been inaccessible even to our violinists of today. David, together with Joachim, the former by his editing and the latter by his concert programmes created a pattern to which nearly all our present-day violin recital programmes conform. David grouped his editing of these standard works into *the Hohe Schule des Violinspiels*—a work that 'marks an epoch in the development of modern violin playing'. Vitali's *Ciaccona* and *Corelli's Folies d'Espagne* (Breitkopf Edition) belong to this violin school and are probably the most popular pieces in the collection.

Nearly every violin student must have learnt these two masterpieces. They both sound such essentially violinistic pieces that I feel tempted to warn viola players to leave them strictly alone. To any viola student, however, who has not previously learnt either on the violin they can be recommended for study in the viola version, though it is doubtful if the public performance of these arrangements is desired. Both are celebrated violin classics, the Vitali being an astonishing piece of music for its period and a worthy forerunner of Bach's celebrated Chaconne. In these two works the student will find sufficient practice in every variety of bowings to keep him busy for many months.

There are two sonatas by Nardini that are well worth knowing. That in F minor in the Cranz edition is a fine piece of music. Some of the passages are a little awkward on the viola and as there is a considerable amount of editing still to be added to the printed version in the way of fingering and bowing only advanced students should study it without the guidance of an experienced teacher. The other Nardini sonata is in D and from David's school in the Breitkopf edition. This sonata is longer and on a much bigger scale than any I have discussed up till now. It is excellent fiddling with just a touch of virtuosity about it. The fast movements are not quite so effective on the viola but the slow movements make up for any deficiencies in this respect. The fast movements contain some printed up–bow staccato which is better avoided, and in these days when vibrato plays such an important part in giving intensity to the expression, the printed natural harmonies at the climaxes of the slow movements will instinctively be changed to stopped notes and played with a strong finger.

Porpora in E, also in the Breitkopf edition and also from David's school introduces us to fugal and polyphonic double-stopping. This is already difficult enough on the violin and some players will find the second movement too heavy technically for the viola even if the allegro is played moderato. It requires very strong fingers to make it come off. This is an interesting sonata in the way that it foreshadows much that Bach used later on—the florid style in the arias, the fugal unaccompanied writing in the second movement, and the chordal progressions played arpeggiando. Be careful to listen and accompany the piano part when it has the theme! The last two movements, Aria and Allegretto, are effective when played apart from the rest of the sonata. They are certainly the two movements that sound best on the viola. The cadenzas at the end of these movements are the first we have discovered in this survey and while effective in themselves introduce a new development of form more appropriate perhaps to the concerto.

As Corelli laid its foundation, Tartini, his true successor as performer and composer, brought the purely Italian sonata to its greatest heights both technically and musically and paved the way for Bach's later developments.

The two examples of Tartini's art I wish to comment upon are Sonata No. 2 in F, (Schott edition) and that in D, (Breitkopf). Both are very difficult, especially the latter, but both in their present arrangement are possible on the viola. They abound in trills and other effects so characteristic of Tartini. To its undoubted advantage David in his edition for the viola of the D major sonata wisely omits some of the cadenzas and double-stopping appearing in the violin part. In this sonata also, the last two movements if played alone form a good concert piece. These sonatas are, of course, in the style of writing and technical layout essentially violin works and except for isolated movements must not be expected to sound quite so well on the viola as in the original.

In the course of this and the previous article in this series I have mentioned and discussed a number of Italian sonatas which have appealed to me either as concert pieces or for teaching purposes. The teacher who wishes to maintain his pupils' interest in this type of composition must give him as great a variety of character as possible in the genre. By studying my remarks the reader will have a rough guide to the respective difficulties and the varying musical conceptions of the principal composers of this epoch. As a foundation for a broad cantabile style combined with a sureness of left hand and bowing technique in the classical tradition, some study of these sonatas is indispensable to the viola student. The list is not by any means exhaustive and, repertoire being mainly an individual preference, the viola player who feels tempted to explore still further this wealth of violin literature will be amply rewarded.

I append a further list of published arrangements for viola and piano which the reader might find useful. It contains several sonatas not previously mentioned in these articles. I have omitted any appearing in foreign editions which might now be difficult to obtain.

Augener[1]:   Handel, in C maj; Grazioli, in F; Marcello, in E minor.

Schott: Ariosti, Nos. 1–6; Boccherini, No.

3; Corelli, No. 12; Francoeur, No. 4; Gavinies, No. 2; Handel, No. 10; Marcello, No. 3; Nardini, No. I; Tartini No. 2; Porpora, No. 9; Abel, in E minor; Pagin, No. S; Leclair, No. 3.

Breitkopf: Biber, in C minor; Porpora, in G; Vivaldi, in A; Leclair, in C minor, and in G; Nardini, in D; Veracini, in E minor; Tartini, in D; Vitali, Ciaccona in G minor; Locatelli, in G minor; Geminiani, in C minor; Corelli, Folies d'Espagne; and three Anonymous, in A minor, in E flat, and C minor.

Peters: Eccles, in G minor.
Cranz: Nardini, in F minor.

(Reprinted from the Strad Magazine, January 1940)

The Sonata from Bach to Brahms

If we care to follow the history of the sonata from the close of the Italian period, which culminated in Bach, we find that the violin suffers a temporary eclipse in favour of the harpsichord and klavier. Just as the development of the early Italian sonata went hand in hand with the development of the violin and violin playing, so now, the successive refinements and inventions make keyboard instruments play their part and almost monopolise the further advance of the sonata.

Bach's sons were conspicuous for their innovations, especially C.P.E.Bach, who, writing about seventy harpsichord sonatas laid the foundation of the modern sonata as we know it. This type of sonata is usually in two or three movements (and much later, in four movements,) contrasted in tempo, mood and key, with at least one movement in 'First Movement Form'. If we trace violin music through this period we find that by the time we come to the sonatas of Haydn, far from being the solo part the violin has lost its predominance and is glad to be tolerated as an accompanying or obbligato part to the harpsichord. This was of course a scheme of things that could not last. Gradually during Haydn's later sonatas, the sonatas of

Mozart and the early Beethoven examples, the violin reasserts itself, till we find in such works as the Kreutzer that the two partners are again on equal terms—and on more or less equal terms they have remained till the present day, so that nowadays every violin and piano sonata is definitely a duet for two soloists.

From the time of the establishment of the modern sonata in the middle of the 18th century up to the late 19th century no sonatas were written for the viola. If we wish to trace the history of viola playing we must study the duos, trios and quartets of the celebrated composers. If we examine the quartets of Haydn, Mozart, Beethoven, Schubert and Brahms we find the history to be one of steady development from the simplest possible part to one of virtuoso attainments. Possibly it was Mozart, who actually played the instrument, who did more than anyone to advance the scope and accomplishment of the viola. Certainly he wrote more works featuring the viola—for instance the violin and viola duets, the *Sinfonia Concertante* for violin and viola, the trio for viola, clarinet and piano and the five quintets with two violas. Schumann who also interested himself in the viola, writing Marchenbilder for viola and piano and other pieces for viola, clarinet and piano was rather less successful in his understanding of the peculiar difficulties inherent in writing for this instrument.

Brahms in his chamber music demands more from the viola in the way of technique and emotional expression than any of his predecessors. That he was interested in the viola as a solo instrument we know from the alternate versions he prepared for viola and piano of his clarinet sonatas and from the two lovely songs with viola obbligato.

Now this survey is not very encouraging to the viola player eager to establish a solo repertoire. Once again, as in my previous survey of earlier music, he is forced to rely on arrangements but with an added difficulty to surmount. Whereas the violin and cello sonatas of the Italian period are all possible on the viola except where technical difficulties of transposition render them inconvenient, these later sonatas are often so bound up with the musical colour of the particular instrument and the pitch at which the music is played that any transposition would so destroy the composer's intention as to become sacrilege on the part of the arranger. Again I must stress that the utmost discretion must be employed in the choice of work the viola player elects to arrange, and even further deliberation before risking a public performance. While no hard and fast rule can be laid down it is advisable, at least for concert performances, to leave the celebrated masterpieces in their original form, and to endeavour to arrange only those works which are, for some reason unconnected with their musical value, rarely performed.

I will now examine some of the sonatas which are available from the period covered by the foregoing historical sketch.

Bach stands at the parting of the ways. He represents the crowning effort of the Italian Sonata and foreshadows the new developments, since he was the first to write out the piano part in full instead of relying on the efforts of the pianist (or editor) guided by a figured bass. He has written three sonatas for viola da gamba and cembalo which are arranged for viola and piano and published by Breitkopf. The piano and cembalo parts are identical. As the viola has not the same compass as the viola da gamba, the music is transposed to an octave higher where it goes below the C string. In addition to this some other phrases are arranged an octave higher for purely artistic reasons, otherwise the player might find himself utilising the C and G strings to the exclusion of the other two. The result would be monotonous. In this edition the slow movements treated thus are excellent. In the quick movements, however, an even bolder policy of placing the viola part in the register at which it sounds best might have brought happier results. It is not enough to make an arrangement of the viola part which is satisfactory in itself, the real test comes when it is played with the piano. This is where I feel the present arrangement might be improved, since many of the quick passages on the lower strings do not come through sufficiently well for the subject matter to stand out. This may be the reason why these sonatas are not so well known amongst viola players as they deserve to be.

The student will be repaid, and incidentally learn a great deal more about the music, by taking pen and paper and endeavouring to make his own arrangement. The scheme is simple in idea but demands great care in execution.

Compare the viola part with the 'cello part (which follows the original closely and is printed over the piano score). Observe where the editor has had to make alterations and, bearing these in mind endeavour to place the solo viola part in the best sounding register even if it means transposing the original two octaves higher! Avoid breaking up a passage by the sudden leap of an octave by changing the register only after a convenient cadence. Remember that Bach, writing for the violin, rarely goes beyond the fourth position on the E string, so the arrangement should use a corresponding compass on the viola.

As regards the musical interpretation it has become the custom for editors to add indiscriminately all kinds of slurs and bowing marks not in Bach's original score and it is impossible to get at the heart of the music till these have been erased. If you compare the opening subjects or the two allegro movements of the first sonata with the original as printed in the Bach Gesellschaft Edition you will find that much of the distinctive character of the themes is lost by the addition of only one or two slurs! An interesting point is to compare your tempo of the Adagio of the first sonata with that of the Andante of the second sonata—there should be a noticeable difference in the quaver pulse. Above all, beware of taking any of the Allegro movements too fast. Bach rarely demands any passage to be played with virtuosity unless he writes in demi–semiquavers. As these sonatas are so seldom heard on the instruments they were written for, there is every excuse for making arrangements and playing them in public.

I shall not mention individually each of the unaccompanied sonatas of Bach. They are all difficult, containing enough study to last a life time, and should be attempted only after the student has mastered some of the easier Kreutzer. As the movements of each sonata vary greatly in degree of difficulty and as they will be used only for study the teacher should commence by giving the pupil a few selected movements rather than a whole sonata. There are six sonatas or suites for violoncello and six for violin. Both sets are arranged for viola and all, with minor adjustments, are possible. I can thoroughly recommend the arrangement of the cello sonatas in the Schirmer Edition. The only viola copy of the violin sonatas I know is rather out of date so I would recommend the viola student to purchase one of the many excellent editions fingered and bowed by any celebrated violin teacher, and read it down a fifth. This means that what is played on the upper string of the violin is performed on the corresponding upper string of the viola with the same fingering and so on. Occasionally chords which are only possible on the violin by extension will be found impossible on the viola and the only solution is to leave out a note, rearrange the chord or play one of the notes as an acciaccatura.

The partitas, which are Nos. 2 and 4 of the violin sonatas will be found to be easier than the others which contain very difficult fugues. If the player has a very strong hand he can try the celebrated Chaconne from the 4th sonata, a viola version of which is published by Augener. In collaboration with Alan Richardson I have made arrangements of the two most popular movements from these sonatas:- the prelude and Gavotte from the 6th sonata. They are published by the Oxford University press, and can be played with or without the piano accompaniment as desired. The sonata for horn and piano by Beethoven is so difficult for the horn that one rarely hears a performance quite free from the technical troubles which often make listening to the horn a somewhat trying experience! We can therefore welcome the arrangement in the Breitkopf Edition. Beethoven wrote this sonata for his own use as a concert pianist so that most of the interesting passage work will be found in the piano part. Nevertheless, although the viola part is comparatively simple the arranger has adapted the horn part in an interesting way. This is a very useful work for amateurs where of the two players the pianist is the more advanced.

Schubert wrote a very fine sonata for arpeggione and piano. The arpeggione was a six stringed instrument which enjoyed a very limited vogue during Schubert's lifetime and is now interesting only as a museum piece. It had a very wide compass—much greater than any present day string instrument—and as it would be a pity never to hear the sonata, various arrangements for cello or viola have been made from time to time. The viola arrangement in the Doblinger edition is quite good, though it hardly exploits the virtuoso element of the original. Besides, viola players are now much more adventurous in the use of the upper register than they were when this arrangement was made. I have recently published a new arrangement of my own.

There is a sonata by Rubinstein which I have always found rather dull. What a pity it is not a better work as it is interesting historically as being the first viola sonata ever to be written and for a long time the only original viola sonata in the repertoire!

The two sonatas by Brahms are so well known that I need not say much about them. Originally written for clarinet, an alternative version for viola with slight alterations was made by Brahms himself. Some of the passages are still essentially clarinet music and the arpeggios and large intervals characteristic of clarinet technique (see the first page of the F minor sonata) will never sound quite so well on the viola. Apart from these exceptions however, it is fine sounding viola music and they are probably the most frequently played sonatas in the repertoire.

(Reprinted from the Strad Magazine, February 1940)

The Concerto in the 18th and 19th Centuries

Now that I have traced the history of the sonata from the earliest times to the beginning of the present century it might be interesting to follow in a similar way the history of its companion piece in sonata form—the concerto.

Although we naturally think of a concerto nowadays as a full length composition, usually in three movements, for a solo instrument playing in a virtuoso style against an orchestral background, the earliest application of the term was rather different. At first it merely denoted several different instruments playing together in consort. By the time we reach the 17th and 18th centuries we find composers like Corelli combining this group of solo instruments with an orchestra. This type of composition was known as a Concerto Grosso. All the violinist composers for some time after this followed Corelli's example, including Handel, who wrote twelve such concertos for two solo violins and one solo cello with string orchestra, and six more for other instrumentations. The most celebrated are the *Brandenburg Concertos* by Bach. Viola players should note the Sixth in B flat for divisi violas where the first and second viola parts replace the usual first and second violins; No. 3 in G for strings only is also interesting, containing as it does three separate viola parts.

It is unfortunate that Corelli wrote his celebrated concertos for two solo violins and cello, omitting the viola, and equally unfortunate that his successors should have followed his example, for this more than anything else delayed the development of the viola as a solo instrument. We have to wait till nearly Haydn's time before the viola takes its place again on equal terms with the others to form the string quartet as we know it. An interesting and equally unfortunate side issue, probably resulting from the same precedent created by Corelli is the scarcity of violas from the great Italian makers between the years 1700 and 1750.

While the concerto grosso, by the number and style of its movements, follows closely the suite and sonata da camera, the violinist–composers, probably for their own personal display evolved a solo concerto more serious in style. This developed in close association with the sonata and symphony, and the concerto proper as we know it today was finally established by Mozart.

With one exception there were no concertos, so far as I can trace, written for the viola. Once again we have to rely on arrangements to supply us with a classical repertoire. From the list of published arrangements we are fortunate in having at least one example to represent the concerto in each period from Handel to Weber. Here is a list, together with the publishers' names, which the reader might find useful for reference:

Handel (1685–1759)
    Concerto in B minor   Max Eschig et Cie. (Paris)
    and   Schott
C.P.E. Bach (1714–1788)
    Concerto in D major   Schirmer (New York)
    Concerto in B flat   Breitkopf
Haydn (1732–1809)

Concerto in D	Breitkopf
Karl Stamitz (1746–1801)	
Concerto Op. 1 in D	Breitkopf and Peters
Mozart (1756 7797)	
Symphonie Concertante	Breitkopf and Peters
(for Violin and Viola)	
(Horn) Concerto	Breitkopf
(Clarinet) Concerto in A	Andre
Weber (1786–1826)	
Andante e Rondo Ungarese	Schott

After this there are no more concertos till modern times; nothing by Beethoven, Schubert, Schumann, Mendelssohn or Brahms is possible in arranged form.

Let me now say something in turn about each concerto from the above list. We are indebted to Henri Casadesus for a great deal of valuable research in old music. He has edited and re-scored much of this to make it possible for us to hear it on modern instruments without in any serious way destroying the original intention of the composer. In 1901 he founded the Collection de Repertoire de la Societé des Instruments Anciens, and it is from this 'Collection Casadesus' that the first two of our concertos are taken.

When I inferred that few viola concertos were written during the 18th and 19th centuries I was doubtful whether the Handel concerto was original or an arrangement. There is nothing on the copy to tell what the original might have been and yet again, by the style and compass of the solo part, it would be hard to imagine Handel writing anything so daring for a solo viola at that time. Original or arrangement it is fine music to practise and to play. It has become very popular in this country in recent years, thanks to the performances by William Primrose and others. The first movement with its broad detached bowing and bold style reminds us somewhat of the Bach double violin concerto. The player may find some of the bowing marks in this movement more awkward than they need be, e.g. the up-bow staccato should be disregarded. The slow movement is a fine Handelian melody and is excellent for tonal practice. I always find the marking *'Allegro molto'* for the last movement rather disturbing, especially as the editor has had to mark a *'piu lento'* half way through to make things possible for the orchestra (or piano). A much more satisfactory arrangement is to play the whole movement Allegro moderato or even Allegretto. I have heard it performed in this way and it seemed to me more correct from a musical point of view.

The concerto by C.P.E. Bach for violin or viola, also from the Collection Casadesus is definitely an arrangement—from the original for viols. This too, is very fine music to play on the viola. The style may remind you of the Vivaldi fiddle concertos—it is broad and spacious. The first movement, despite its marking Allegro moderato should be taken four beats to the bar. The interesting and original slow movement should be first learned by thinking of nine quavers to the bar, circa, = 100, the dotted crochet beat being rather unwieldy at this speed. The tempo and style of the last movement is remarkably similar to the Handel and in this case is rightly marked Allegretto. Here we encounter for the first time a cadenza—formerly a flourish over a 6/4 chord for the soloist before the final cadence; later developments elaborated this into a some times over–long technical display of virtuosity, frequently marred by the triteness of the musical treatment of the original themes. In a concerto of this period I think it is always best to keep the cadenza as short as possible, an arpeggio on the 6/4 chord often being sufficient. By a judicious cut in the tutti one can often avoid the issue altogether. The present ad lib cadenza may be omitted without any serious loss to the concerto as a whole.

The other concerto by C.P.E. Bach in the Breitkopf edition arranged from the original for cello, is also a fine work. As it is now impossible to get any further copies of this work till the end of the war I will pass on to the next on the list.

The Haydn cello concerto in D is such a celebrated war-horse in the cellist's repertoire and is so often performed that the viola player must resign himself to playing this arrangement only in private. Students will find useful practice in the excellent arrangement by Alfred Spitzner—it is just as difficult and interesting technically for the viola as it is in the original. For those who revel in cadenzas there is an excellent one at the end of the first movement included in this edition. That in the last movement is quite unnecessary and the optional cut should be observed. Readers might be interested in a very amusing commentary on this concerto by Tovey in his *'Essays in Musical Analysis'*, Vol. 3.

(*Reprinted from the Strad Magaazine, April 1940*)

The Concerto in the 18th and 19th Centuries
(continued)

Before continuing my survey I should again like to emphasise that I am dealing solely with those concertos which are printed in editions easily obtained. Many more viola concertos were written during this period than appear on my list, but time and the wise forbearance of editors has confined them to oblivion. If the various specimens I have seen in MS. or rare editions are any guide, I doubt if many master pieces are yet to be discovered .

The Stamitz concerto, Op. 1, is next on our list. This is interesting as being possibly our one and only original concerto for the viola from the period covered by this article. Stamitz himself was known as a performer on the viola and viola d'amore besides being also a composer of note, and the concerto is written throughout with a complete understanding of the instrument. There are various differences between the Breitkopf and Peters edition, the latter which includes it in a volume called *'Alte Meister des Violaspiels'* being the more accurate. In the Breitkopf edition the editor, Paul Klengel, has been tempted to try to improve on the original by rewriting some passages in thirds which, besides making very awkward double-stopping, lie too low to be really effective. Until I discovered the Peters edition this and other passages made me wonder if this concerto were not also an arrangement after all—perhaps from an original for viola d'amore. As usual the less an editor changes, the better the result. It is pleasant, if undistinguished music. Teachers will find this work useful, especially for younger students who will enjoy it, until experience makes them realise how much better Mozart could do the same type of thing.

This brings us to the consideration of Mozart's works. The *Symphonie Concertante* for violin and viola is the nearest

Mozart came to writing a solo viola concerto. Although in this work the viola has to share honours with the solo violin we are greatly indebted to Mozart for such a fine work for it remains far and away the most important composition for the viola up to the beginning of the present century. The combination of violin and viola is one that seems to have attracted Mozart as he also wrote two unaccompanied duets for the same combination. Mozart was certainly the first of the great composers to realise all the latent possibilities of the viola as a solo instrument.

For some strange reason the viola part of this concerto is written in D major, and as the concerto is in E flat the viola has to be tuned up a semitone. This savours rather of Paganini than Mozart! Why he did it is hard to tell. perhaps he aimed at a greater brilliance than the viola was capable of giving at that time. As pitch has risen since Mozart's day and the improved strings now available have all tended towards making the viola more brilliant, there does not now seem the same necessity for this special tuning. In any case all the notes are possible whether the viola is tuned to A or B flat. Breitkopf publish the viola part with the special tuning in D and Peters have the part as it would normally appear in E flat. Both versions are equally difficult and, I think, equally effective, so I leave the choice to the player. It is certain that the constant tuning of the viola up and down a semitone in order to practise the part is most disturbing to the instrument, and where steel strings are used on a fine old Italian instrument the added tension is a definite risk.

Mozart has himself supplied an excellent cadenza for the first movement which requires none of the additions and embellishments one so often hears at public performances to make it effective. The slow movement is usually considered sufficiently long without a cadenza and I wish to recommend the usual practice of making a small cut in the tutti from the close of the solo parts to eight bars from the end.

The Horn concerto of Mozart is useful only for teaching purposes. The Clarinet concerto on the other hand is an exceedingly interesting composition being one of the last works he completed. Possibly because Brahms rearranged his clarinet sonatas for viola, players are apt to favour any clarinet piece in arrangement. This of course is not always possible, but here in Mozart's work a very satisfactory result can be obtained. The unnamed arranger in André's edition has been over-bold I think in rearranging some typical clarinet passages to suit viola technique. In a work of this importance it is better to keep to Mozart's original except where it is obviously impossible. Viola players will enjoy this work tremendously.

It only remains to mention the nine-minute work by Weber. In a note in the Schott edition it states that Weber composed this work for his brother Fritz. Later he rewrote the work for bassoon, which is the version in which it is usually heard. It is not a great work, being rather trivial in places. Teachers will find it useful for younger students, who will probably be the only people to take it seriously.

Before concluding our consideration of the concerto, mention might be made of one other interesting work—the Berlioz Symphony, *Harold in Italy*. There is conflicting evidence about the origin of this work, some authorities maintain that it was originally commissioned by Paganini as a viola concerto and some even assure us that Paganini actually gave the first performance. Whatever the true story may be, the resulting work is certainly not a concerto. True, it has a very important solo viola part—best described as an obbligato. If we regard the symphony as one of Berlioz's usual excursions into virtuoso feats of orchestration—an example well in keeping with his bizarre and extravagant imagination—we can discount the legends and examine the work as the programme music it really is. The writing for the viola is effective, but its treatment is often purely that of an orchestral colour—viz. the sardonic effect of the arpeggios played ponticello. While it is difficult to imagine Paganini taking a really active interest in the work, it is nevertheless important to us as an indication of the growing desire to exploit the characteristic tonal qualities of the viola.

This ends the survey of the concerto up to modern times. I will next examine some of the masterpieces of the present century when the real history of the solo viola repertoire begins.

(Reprinted from the Strad Magazine, May 1940)

The English Viola Sonata

Two hundred years of continuous experiment has wrought many changes on the sonata as an art form. The process has been one of steady advancement from the simplest origins to a structure of magnificent complexity and divergence of idea. It is at once the vehicle for expressing the most profound intellectual thoughts of musicians and the means of conveying in the most readily acceptable form instrumental music lasting an appreciable length of time.

From being a piece written with some restraint in regard to the chamber music tradition, it now employs every technical resource and means of expression formerly reserved for the concerto. The modern violin sonata has often the air of a concerto for two instruments without orchestra .

The technical advances in violin playing and teaching were reflected in the way of writing for that instrument, and although the viola remained undisturbed as a solo instrument during most of these developments, the first compositions to appear early in this century took full account of the results achieved on the violin. These new works immediately transfer the virtuoso element to the viola. Although it might be said that the technique of violin playing had been analysed and mastered to the highest degree, the effect of these works on the majority of viola players must have been shattering. The full compass of the instrument was at once exploited, and effects of double stopping and bowing were also borrowed from the violin and featured. Not all these technical displays were unqualified in their success, and although some have since been discarded, the experiments were justified in bringing about a definite style of writing for the viola.

The English composers, inspired by Lionel Tertis's performances, lead the way in the new adventure of discovering the solo viola and did great service in finally dispelling the feeling of inferiority under which the instrument had laboured for so long. It is fortunate for the viola that during this period England has been producing some of its greatest composers—figures who can equal in achievement the output of their continental rivals. Their general style of composition, while remaining indisputably English in character conforms to no definite schools such as we find on the continent. While certainly learning from each other, and also imitating the modernistic tendencies of the more advanced schools, they have contrived to keep their individuality without going to extremes. The collection and study of folk song has had a marked effect on some, while the revival of interest in the madrigal school and the great period of Tudor music has also been a definite influence.

Almost every living English composer of note has some major viola work to his credit. Bax, Bliss, Vaughan Williams and Walton are the names that most readily spring to mind, and if I confine my remarks in this article to the Sonatas and Suites of some of the less well known composers it is with the desire that by understanding their contributions we may more fully appreciate the other masterpieces.

York Bowen and Benjamin Dale were probably the first in the field. York Bowen has given us two sonatas, No. 1 in C minor and No. 2 in F, of which probably No. 1 is the better music. It is certainly the more popular. In style it is both lyrical and romantic and abounds in delightful touches. It is technically difficult but exceedingly well written for the instrument, York Bowen having enjoyed the undoubted advantage of being able to play the viola himself. It is simple, happy music, easy to listen to and with the right amount of technical display to carry it along and hold the interest of players. To any violinist with a fairly advanced technique who may be interested in trying the viola, it forms an ideal piece for the experiment. It is equally interesting from the pianist's point of view. This work should certainly be in every viola player's repertoire.

No. 2 in F has never enjoyed the same popularity. It closely follows the style and general design of the earlier work as though it had been written in imitation of the previous success. It is in consequence a less inspired work. Nevertheless it too is good music, though more difficult and not quite so grateful to play. Any player who is at all doubtful of the upper register of the viola will soon find himself in difficulties. Both works ably dispel the accusation that viola players can only play slow and gloomy music.

There are also two works by Dale for viola and piano. Let me first deal with the *Phantasy*, Op. 4. This is very difficult both musically and technically, requiring a great deal of joint rehearsal. Each partner must know both parts intimately for the full appreciation of the music and for its successful performance. It is much more serious music than the York Bowen works, demanding a firmer technique and a more solid style of playing. Yet it is romantic music and very exciting to play, making full use as it does of all kinds of legitimate viola effects of tone colour. It is music that some people might unfortunately find dated—a trifle old-fashioned. It belongs to a period of music that is almost too near for us to appreciate against its historical background. But it is certainly music that will find a lasting place in the viola repertoire. For a phantasy work—that is, it is played from beginning to end without a pause—it is long, perhaps over–long, and yet the best compliment to its structure is the difficulty anyone would experience in finding a workable cut that would not destroy the form.

The other work by Dale, the Suite Op. 2, is on an even larger scale. Whether the viola is capable of sustaining the interest during a work that takes over half an hour to perform is doubtful, but its extreme length should not deter viola players from adding it to the repertoire as it is fine music throughout. Perhaps the most successful movement is the lovely Romance. Certainly it is one of the most popular pieces in the repertoire and can be performed apart from the rest of the Suite. It is the most successful of all Dale's compositions. In this Suite, more so than in any of the previous works discussed in this article we are aware of technical devices borrowed from what is really essentially violin technique. Not all of it is easy to bring off on the viola. It is, of course, unnecessary and foolhardy for the viola in any way to enter into competition with the violin with technical displays in the upper register. There are legitimate and more characteristic methods at its disposal. This is a work for advanced students and performers only, though some amateurs may find the Romance within their attainments. A novelty worth mentioning is the *Introduction and Andante* for six violas by the same composer. Dale in these viola works and his other compositions of this period contributed much that was thoughtful and highly original to the art of composition. It was indeed unfortunate that his career was interrupted by internment in Germany during the 1914-1918 war.

Amateurs and performers alike will be grateful for the pleasant and melodious music by Richard Walthew. Written in a style that might be considered reminiscent of Victorian composition it requires no apology for the unadventurousness of its aims. It is the music of a well-ordered mind which has pleasant things to say and knows how to say them and how to write them aptly in terms of the instruments employed. It belongs to a school of English composition that could well stand a revival; indeed, it might act as a tonic to the musical world surfeited by some of the ugly complexities and dissonances of the modern school. There are two sonatas: one the *Serenade–Sonata*, an early work, and the second in D, a comparatively recent work which I have edited myself. Both are short and concise and of much the same degree of difficulty.

Other works which the reader might care to note are the sonata by Granville Bantock (recently revised and shortened by the composer), and a sonata by Ernest Walker. This latter was one of the earliest examples of the English viola sonata from the period covered by this article. There is an interesting Suite by Theodore Holland, the viola part of which I have also edited. This work, while presenting no involved musical problems is great fun to play, the last movement in particular being full of good spirit. The Romance is a beautiful piece of music and may be played separately from the rest of the suite. The difficulties throughout the work are interesting technically and well worth any amount of practice since they are all characteristic of the instrument, as is only to be expected from a composer who knows the viola from the player's point of view.

(Reprinted from the Strad Magazine, June 1940)

The English Viola Sonata
(continued)

No one has done more towards establishing a permanent viola repertoire than Sir Arnold Bax. Both by his thorough knowledge of the viola's capabilities and by the number of important works he has contributed he has, by example, gone far to form a definite style of writing for the instrument.

It may truthfully be said that almost alone among our celebrated living composers Bax enjoys a greater reputation for his chamber music works than for his orchestral or choral compositions. His list of chamber music is formidable, including as it does, three string quartets, a double viola quintet, a piano quartet and quintet, a nonet, an oboe quintet, etc., etc., besides sonatas for piano, violin and piano and cello and piano.

The sonata for viola and piano is a truly magnificent work. It should be in every viola player's repertoire—that is, for those who can manage to play it, as it is exceedingly difficult. For those who find it beyond their powers there are excellent records by William Primrose and Harriet Cohen. It is unusual in construction having a rhapsodic first movement, an energetic second movement containing a *piu lento* tune, and a very slow contemplative third movement. Notice how the whole is knit together by the continually recurring three–note motive, which first appears at the very beginning of the sonata. This is a favourite device of Bax as we shall see. Listen to the lovely tunes in this and the second movement—tunes which have an engaging Celtic flavour about them. Indeed the whole sonata is characterised by a decided Irish feeling, which reaches its climax in the veiled mysticism of the last movement. As in all Bax's greater works we are never conscious of the masterly technique which seizes upon the mood and expresses it so well in the terms of the instruments employed. We can only admire such amazing results as the quiet mystery at the beginning and end of the first movement, the almost satanic ferocity at the beginning of the second, examples multiply and we must refer the reader to the score itself for the full comprehension of this masterpiece.

A slighter composition by the same composer is the *Legende* for viola and piano. It packs a great deal of drama into a very short space. The mood alternates between one of terrific intensity and one of poetic calm. In many ways it reminds me of the piano quartet in its uncompromising outlook. Unfortunately for some it is again beyond the scope of all but the most accomplished players.

Reference must now he made to Bax's writing for another

instrument not usually in great demand for solo playing—the Harp. It is of special importance to us, as one of his best chamber music works, the *Phantasy Sonata*, is written for viola and harp. Not everyone will have the opportunity of playing this, since although good viola players are scarce, good harp players are exceedingly rare, and the harpist has to be very good to play this music. Bax spent a considerable time studying the harp technique and its possibilities as a solo instrument; the harp Quintet, *Elegiac Trio* for flute, viola and harp and the present sonata are the results.

It was a bold idea to bring together these two neglected instruments, the harp and viola, and write for them a work of this magnitude, for although it is called a *Phantasy Sonata* (which usually refers to a one movement work, or at least one demanding continuous performance from beginning to end) this is really a full length sonata in four movements, with only slight breaks. In any case, during a work lasting about twenty five minutes, some opportunities for tuning both the harp and viola would be essential. Again we have a motif in varied form recurring in each movement, binding the whole together. This time the motif is not a short figure as in the viola and piano sonata, but a whole phrase. This sonata is full of characteristic touches, the rhapsodic first movement with its changing tempi, the elaborate decoration of the slow movement woven around the wistful sustained melody, and the Irish rhythms of the last movement. An unusual feature is the *grazioso scherzo*, a happy movement with a lilting waltz rhythm. It is founded on the same recurring motive which is again used in the coda to the whole work, where the music rises to a truly noble dignity. The combination of harp and viola is treated with such success that it is astonishing no other composer has imitated this example. Probably the difficulty of getting together performers of these two unusual solo instruments has deterred them.

If these works by Bax are so difficult that they are beyond your powers as a performer, the same will certainly be the case in the sonata by Arthur Bliss. This must surely be the most difficult sonata yet written for the viola. As it is also musically difficult may I be excused if I mention my recording of the work with Myers Foggin for Decca, which may help you towards a quicker understanding and appreciation? Do not be put off this work by judging it adversely at a first hearing, as it is the most angular music, full of the strangest idioms, odd trills and false relations, but persevere in your listening and you will certainly be rewarded—and surprised too, when you find this strange music taking shape and really becoming very fascinating. The first movement is the most difficult to discover. The second movement with its ghostly atmospheric beginning and ending contains the best music. It is powerful and dramatic. The third movement, a *Furiant*, a term probably borrowed from Dvorak, is a lively affair full of energy and boisterous spirits. The sonata ends with a prolonged Coda, which in referring to some of the themes appearing earlier, sums up the whole and brings it to a triumphant conclusion. Throughout the viola part there are included various alternative versions, special fingerings and passages intended to be played on a particular string. Not all of these difficulties need be included for a full realisation of the music. So much depends on the individual technique of the performer, the size of hand, and, as always in dealing with the viola, the characteristics of the particular instrument, e.g., most players will take the *'ossia'* version at the end of the *Furiant*. Again, owing to the steep curve of the bridge required on the viola most of the four-note chordal passages are better if treated with discretion. There is something Byronic in the romanticism which inspired this work. It has a quality which suits the slightly nasal timbre of the viola. How full and sonorous it all sounds, but notice how thin the texture looks in the score–a tribute to the composer's knowledge of how to write for his instruments. This must rank among the foremost of the viola works of the modern English school.

Publishers in general are to be congratulated on their enterprise in printing so many of these viola sonatas. The sale is unfortunately limited by the scarcity of viola players, but their number is steadily growing and it is to be hoped that this will act as an encouragement to publishers to continue their adventurous policy.

In addition to the works already mentioned there are many modern English sonatas still in manuscript. I can mention sonatas by Walter Leigh, Alan Paul, Elizabeth Maconchy Alan Rawsthorne, J.B. McEwen, Cyril Scott and

Arnold Cooke. Of these the last named has I believe been recently published by the Oxford University Press. Walter Leigh and Alan Paul have since won fame in lighter music. The Maconchy is available for hire in the Hinrichsen edition.

If it is true to say that every living composer of note has a viola work to his credit it is equally true of composers who have not yet climbed to prominence. So great has been this sudden awakening of interest that viola players are now constantly being offered first performances of new MS. works. It is indeed a healthy sign and augurs well for the future of the instrument. With so many modern English sonatas to choose from (and this list does not claim to be complete) it would seem almost ungallant to start arranging modern English violin or cello works and adding unnecessarily to the list. I feel it is advisable to gain a thorough knowledge of the viola repertoire of original works before studying any arrangements of modern works. It is interesting, however, to keep trace of new works appearing for violin or cello. Although those players who are keen on arranging music for the viola will find their best and most useful results in music of the past, it is possible to keep abreast of recent developments by learning the new violin or cello works through arrangements for the viola. There is no demand, however, for the public performance of these works, the musical public rightly feeling that if the composer had thought of the work in terms of the viola, there is now sufficient incentive for him to write for that instrument.

Of the many arranged sonatas the most important among the published ones are the violin sonatas Nos. 2 and 3 by Delius, published by Boosey & Hawkes. I believe I am right in saying that Lionel Tertis arranged these in collaboration with the composer. At least the arrangements had the composer's sanction. I am still convinced that these sonatas are better in their original form, the violin tone seeming necessary to their realisation. No. 2 is the more successful, No. 3 having some very awkward skips on the A string. As of course we have nothing in the viola repertoire from Delius, they have their value.

I have now completed the survey of the 20th century English viola sonata and it might be best to examine next the English concertos of the same period.

(Reprinted from the Strad Magazine, August 1940)

The Modern English Viola Concerto

Viola players are fortunate in having in their list of modern English concertos a work which would be an important addition to any instrument's repertoire; a work which may yet prove to be the greatest contribution in concerto style written during the epoch. I refer to the Viola Concerto by William Walton. This had its first performance in 1929 by Paul Hindemith. It was written when the composer was about twenty seven, and is the first of the series of important works (*Belshazzar's Feast, 1931, Symphony, 1935, Violin Concerto, 1939*) which established Walton as a composer of world renown. Each work, highly individual, with a personality of its own, is the result of careful and deliberate thought, often extended over a considerable period. But though Walton writes slowly, a survey of his work shows no academic heaviness of thought but rather a spontaneity of invention and wit, most obviously displayed in such works as *Portsmouth Point, Facade* and the second movement of this concerto. The three movements, though contrasted in tempo, have a unity of idea if not of mood. The first movement is slow, the second very vigorous and rhythmic, while the third, though marked Allegro, soon returns to the broad lyrical mood of the first movement. There is a sombre note in the quieter moments of this work which suits admirably the tonal characteristics of the viola. As to the syncopated jazz rhythms of the second movement, with the solo part scurrying about at (for the viola) breakneck speed, there are things here which no viola player ever had to do before! It is calculated to keep both performers and listeners continually on the alert.

The work is published by the Oxford University Press in a version for viola with piano, though no piano could possibly give an adequate account of the richness of the orchestral score either in its delicate colouring or in its tremendous climaxes. The viola part, edited by Lionel Tertis, unfortunately differs in some respects from the solo version printed in the piano copy. Later, William Primrose still further edited the viola part—but that the piano copy represents the composer's true intentions is finally confirmed by the miniature score recently published by O.U.P. and the set of records made under the composer's personal supervision by Frederick Riddle (Decca, X 199–201.)

The Concerto is frankly modern, one of the most 'advanced' works for the viola. Because it refuses to express its message in a familiar idiom, because it may be difficult to understand, and just because it is so new and so essentially a product of our own age, do not therefore misjudge it hastily. That would be a mistake, for emphatically, it is a masterpiece.

Vaughan Williams is another great English composer who has given the viola a welcome addition to its concerto repertoire—albeit in a rather unusual and individual form. The Suite for viola and orchestra is a series of short pieces, mostly dances, such as we find in Bach, but treated in a modern fashion. Thus we have a *Prelude*, a *Christmas Dance*, *Moto Perpetuo*, *Polka Melancolique*, etc. eight pieces in all. The Suite is still further original in its design in that the eight pieces are bracketed together to form three separate groups. Each group is complete in itself, the pieces being nicely contrasted in tempo and style, but in no way linked by musical 'idea.' In fact, in an actual performance of the suite as a whole, one is in no way aware of this grouping, which points to the fact that this said grouping is quite arbitrary and of no musical significance. It is a very useful scheme of things, however, since, no matter how well the Suite as a whole comes off with orchestra, when performed with piano the player will be best advised to include only a single group in a programme. The version for full orchestra is very delicately scored and enables the viola to stand out without effort. It is evident that the composer sanctions a performance with either orchestral or piano accompaniment. Since it is impossible to transfer all the musical score to the pianoforte this version has one or two of the orchestral passages played by the solo viola.

Most players will favour the first group, Prelude, Carol and Christmas Dance. It is probably the easiest group and further, presents Vaughan Williams in his most characteristic vein. He is essentially an English composer, the influence of

153

English Folk Song and English Tudor music being so apparent in all his works, that it constitutes both an asset and a liability; an asset in that he has an enormous following among those who know and love the tradition and a liability in that many people especially on the continent, have absolutely no point of contact in coming to an understanding of his music.

The second group contains the Moto Perpetuo, which will present difficulties of execution impossible to all but the most advanced players. In the third group we rediscover in the *Musette* the same loveable personality that was first revealed in the *Carol* and *Ballad*, while nothing could be more exhilarating than the bustling *Galop* which brings the Suite to a close.

There has been a tendency among English composers to favour the one movement concerto. This is probably an off-shoot of the Fantasy Sonata encouraged by W.W. Cobbett in his numerous competitions. I would like to mention three such concertos—a *Phantasy* by Arnold Bax, a Concerto by Gordon Jacob and a *Rhapsody* by W.H. Reed. Each in its own particular way reflects a facet of English music. To deal with them in that order, the Bax is typical, reminding us of the viola sonatas, a combination of wistful Irish melody and rustic good humour. For a one-movement concerto this is long, playing for some eighteen minutes. It is unfortunately not very successful with piano—that part, a faithful reduction from the score, being particularly ungrateful to play. It indicates the instrumentation and is therefore ideal for practice. Unfortunately this work is rarely performed— I have not myself heard it with orchestra.

Like all his work, the Concerto of Gordon Jacob displays the mind of a sound musician. It is a vigorous work that suits well the rugged quality of the viola. For a concerto it is not over difficult, the only awkward passages lying fairly well under the hand. It is above all a useful work for advanced students.

I am particularly fond of the *Rhapsody of* W.H. Reed. It is on a much smaller scale than either of the two preceding works, and is also much easier to play. It would form an ideal work for introducing the student to the modern English school. It is charming music very effectively written for the instrument.

154

Elgar, our greatest composer, left no viola concerto, but the Concerto for Violoncello has been arranged and is published by Novello. No one who really knows the concerto in its original form can tolerate a performance of the arrangement, even though conceding that this has been cleverly done. The work is essentially bound up with cello tone and technique. Let us recognise this at once and then enjoy practising the work for our own pleasure. There are not so many viola concertos that we can afford to neglect such opportunities of getting acquainted with one of the masterpieces of cello literature. This then concludes the review of the principal English concertos in the viola repertoire. Considering the short period during which the viola has been recognised as a solo instrument it is a repertoire of which we may be justly proud, and performers must be grateful to the modern English composer for what he has done to second them in their cause. Of the major works there remains now only one aspect of the viola repertoire I have yet to discuss, and that is the modern sonatas and concertos of the European school.

(Reprinted from the Strad Magazine, October 1940)

Modern European Sonatas

In a previous article I have remarked on the tremendous influence certain virtuoso players have had when they could also write for their instrument. The history of violin playing is most remarkable in this respect. The names Corelli, Tartini, Paganini, all signified the beginning of new developments, each experimented to discover new and improved ways of playing the instrument, and each added typical works to the violin repertoire, incorporating the new ideas of technique. Later virtuosi, such as Vieuxtemps, Wieniawski and Sarasate, further exploited the technical capacities of the instrument. When the viola came to the forefront as a solo instrument, it took over all these technical devices, or at least as many as it could manage (fingered octaves and tenths, for instance, are best left alone) but it was only after a quarter of a century that composers and players began to realise what sounded effective and what, though possible, was best avoided. The need for a virtuoso player who could also compose was becoming necessary to crystallise the best ideas into a definite style of writing for the viola when Paul Hindemith appeared to fill the gap.

Born in 1895, Hindemith was first a violinist and later the viola player in the Amar String Quartet. While this quartet was winning a name for itself for the interpretation of modern music, its viola player was gaining a name as a composer of the most advanced European school. It would be interesting to study his theories of composition (neo-classicism and atonality) as exemplified in his works, but for the present purpose I must limit my considerations to what most concerns us—his viola music.

Everyone seems to agree that he writes more effectively for the viola than for the violin, and anyone who has heard him perform would certainly say that the style of his playing is definitely characteristic of the viola. He has written numerous works for his instrument, the most notable being the Sonata, Op. 11 No. 4 and a new sonata (1939) for viola and piano Op. 11 No. 5 and Op. 25 No. 1 for viola solo; a Viola Concerto with small chamber orchestra, and one with full orchestra; *Trauermusik* for viola and strings.

Traurmusik is by far the easiest introduction to his music the viola student will find. It was written on the death of King George V when Hindemith was due to broadcast a viola concerto, but writing at great speed completed and performed this piece instead. It is in four short contrasted sections to be played continuously. Technically it is not overly difficult and an adequate performance is possible with piano.

In considering the Sonatas, Op. 11 No. 4 should be the first choice. It is hardly a sonata in the accepted form, but really a Fantasia and Theme with variations. Hindemith calls the Fantasia the first movement and the Theme and first few variations the second movement, while the last few variations with the coda are labelled Finale. As it is directed, in a note by the composer, that the Sonata should be performed in one continuous movement, the listener will be quite unaware of these divisions. Like most of his music this Sonata is fairly difficult to understand at a first hearing.

Even so, it contains none of the extreme ugliness one might expect from modern music—in fact after the student has familiarised himself with the idiom he will be surprised to remember he ever thought it strange. True, there are all the dissonances one expects, the continually changing time signatures, and in one instance an odd key signature, F and G being sharp, but not C—the signature quite justifying itself. But here is also much that is beautiful, a capricious and humorous touch that is very welcome and a stimulating rhythmic feeling, occasionally borrowing from jazz. This sonata is difficult for both performers.

On the whole, Hindemith's viola works are not yet played as much as they deserve in this country—the concertos having had few performances other than those given by Hindemith himself. Whether there is a large public for the unaccompanied sonatas is doubtful, but they deserve the student's attention. They are magnificent practice and clearly owe a great deal to the Bach unaccompanied sonatas. The thought is concise and if occasionally austere, the music is never dull. It is to be hoped that gramophone records of his music will one day be available to help a larger public towards its appreciation. He has written a considerable and varied amount which by its adventurous probing into modern problems has opened up a new school of thought which deserves attention.

Another European composer who will interest viola players is Ernest Bloch. His Viola Suite is considered by Ernest Newman to be the most important work in our repertoire. Bloch as a composer is interesting from several points of view. As a Jew, most of his music is characterised by strong racial traits and his work has an oriental colouring and feeling for atmosphere which is highly favoured by the modern impressionistic school.

Bloch enjoys the undoubted advantage of being able to play the violin, so we find in his attitude towards writing for the viola that he is never at a loss for the means to an end. Thus in the Suite, all the virtuoso accomplishments of harmonics, double-stopping, ponticello, etc., are used in the most effective way. Notice too, how the various melodies are placed to give the viola a chance to sing in its best register. In this particular suite each of the four movements are supposed to represent a different country; but the composer wisely left the movements without their titles, preferring that the music should speak for itself.

The Suite is for viola and piano and the composer later orchestrated the piano part, thus reversing the usual practice of reducing the orchestral score. Strange music, this, and not easy to grasp until you have heard it many times. Performances are not yet numerous, although it has been broadcast on several occasions. In 1937 a Bloch Society was formed in London with a view to encouraging the performance of his works and there are now records of the piano quintet which may help you towards a better understanding of the man and his music.

The viola sonata of Arthur Honegger is not, unfortunately, representative of the composer at his best. Like Bloch, Honegger is of Swiss nationality. He is best known for his sensational works—the locomotive tone poem *Pacific 231* and the football one—*Rugby*. The viola sonata is an early work. The first movement stands apart from the other two by a curious divergence in style. It is extremely modern in feeling and in the harmonic texture—some of the passages in the piano part do not fall into any familiar chordal or keyboard pattern, which makes it exceedingly difficult to learn, while the viola part is full of awkward leaps, for which it is not always possible to find a convenient fingering. Like many other modern piano scores there seem to be so many notes to play that the metronome markings inevitably have to be reduced in speed with a consequent loss to the music. The second and third movements are simple by comparison. They are pleasant, tuneful and easy to understand, the last movement in particular being a joy to play, with its broad vigorous bow strokes. An unequal sonata, but one well worth having in our repertoire. Less advanced players should omit the first movement and concentrate on the other two.

European composers have not given so much attention to writing for the viola as the English. There are few other major works in sonata form worthy of much attention, but here are some that have interested me: There is a sonata by Kornauth—a youthful work written in the over–romantic style of the beginning of this century. As was the custom of European composers of that period, the markings are not written in Italian, but in the composer's own language, which means a tedious half-hour for those unacquainted with it. Hindemith, too, still indulges in this unnecessary habit. The sonata is pleasant music to play and to listen to, and well deserves an occasional performance.

From Italy we have a sonata by Perrota which is not a very distinguished addition to the repertoire. Viola students desirous of getting to know some work of the modern Italian school will be better advised to study the excellent arrangement of Pizzetti's cello sonata. It is an interesting work, difficult, and probably more enjoyable for the players than the audience.

There is one other work I would like to mention—this time from Spain. The *Scene Andalouse,* for solo viola with accompaniment for piano and string quartet, by Turina. This picturesque little work is one of the most fascinating of the modern compositions. It is unpretentious music with all the charm of the Spanish national idiom combined with the facility of writing characteristic of the French school of Ravel and Debussy. It further has the advantage of being a concerto in style without requiring the expensive item of a full orchestra for performance. In this respect it is similar to the concerto for solo violin, piano and string quartet Op. 21 by Chausson, a useful idea which might with advantage be copied by other composers. You will find it easier than most of the other compositions discussed in this article.

I have now reviewed most of the principal major works in the viola repertoire and I hope in a later article to list some of the shorter solos and arrangements.

(Reprinted from the Strad Magazine, December 1940)

Short Solos for the Viola

How often has it happened that the music student whether studying at a school of music or privately, spends his years hard at work on studies, sonatas and concertos, perhaps with the object of an examination for a diploma or degree in view, only to find to his dismay that when he is asked to contribute a few solos at a local concert he has literally nothing to play! Concertos and sonatas may undoubtedly be his best material for advancing him in his technical accomplishments and his knowledge of music, but he must soon realise that it is not every audience that can appreciate them, nor every occasion that demands them. No one can continually wrestle with the biggest things in music without wishing to relax occasionally, so please do not scorn the lesser things. There is, after all, just as much art required to bring off a miniature in a beautiful way, as anyone who has heard Kreisler or Casals will admit. Nor need the student spoil his art or unduly play down to the gallery, for have not all the great masters left an abundance of short pieces for him to choose from? Any student who has had a good schooling in the classical concertos and sonatas may well be left to make his own choice in this department of repertoire.

Now, whereas pianists, violinists, and even cellists have each a large and well known repertoire to choose from, the poor viola player is not yet in such a happy position, and the student may well require some guidance as to what is available. Here are indeed many more viola pieces than one would at first imagine, but they do require finding and sorting out, and it is my purpose here to give a critical survey of some of the music the average player might find useful. There are two ways of tackling the problem: (1) pieces actually written for the viola, and (2) Arrangements.

Owing to the limited sale of viola music not all the pieces which I personally enjoy playing have been published (and this applies in particular to a great deal of very fine modern English music), yet, even so, publishers on the whole are to be congratulated on the enterprise they have already shown in helping to establish a repertoire.

From the classics Schumann is the only one of the great masters who has given us anything at all—*Four Fairy pictures*, Op. 113. These are still played, though they can hardly be called very good Schumann or very good viola music. They were written long before the viola had come to the fore as a solo instrument, and perhaps in consequence they do not show off the viola to its best advantage. Schumann's understanding of writing for strings, especially in his chamber music works, was very limited, as anyone who has studied the piano quartet or quintet is only too well aware. The pieces will probably always remain in the repertoire because of Schumann's name, and therefore may deserve the occasional performance they receive. *Three Hebrew Melodies* by Joachim also have a certain importance in the repertoire. Here the writing for the viola is much better, but the piano accompaniments always strike me as being a little ungainly. There still remains something a little unsatisfactory—the viola has not yet found itself. No. 3 of this set is the best. Joachim's music as a whole is now rarely performed.

The two pieces by Wolstenholme, *Allegretto and Romance*, must have been among the first pieces to have been written and published for the viola and also to have enjoyed a wide popularity. They are charming and tuneful and must surely be in every amateur viola player's repertoire. They date from about 1900. The '*Allegretto*' is the greater favourite of the two. They both seem to lie naturally in the viola register, but will nevertheless require careful fingering by the teacher, as there are one or two awkward moments where fifths across the strings could be troublesome. These pieces deserve the strongest recommendation.

Not quite so successful are a set of *Three Salon pieces by* Rubinstein, although they will prove useful for teachers. Other pieces worth studying are the *Elegy*, Op. 30, by Vieuxtemps, about the only piece from this virtuoso school, and the *Romance*, Op. 85 by Max Bruch.

Coming to modern times, Howard Ferguson has written *Four Pieces*. Although originally for clarinet, they are also available for viola, and in that version are more difficult musically than technically. They are short, intimate mood pictures playing about a minute each and published by Boosey & Hawkes. The same publisher also gives us *Four Pieces* by Frederick Kell. These too are published for clarinet or viola, but in this case the clarinet wins. Most of the writing is so essentially clarinet technique that the viola cannot hope to give more than a makeshift performance of these fine pieces.

During the course of this survey the reader will be struck by the number of pieces written for 'either clarinet or viola.' This seems to be a fairly well established practice nowadays, thanks to Brahms having set the fashion. It is not always happy in its results, at least not from the viola player's point of view. Composers do not always take sufficient care when preparing the viola version to rewrite the passages more obviously for clarinet technique, in terms of the viola. Quick, slurred arpeggios in particular, and sudden leaps of more than an octave in melodic passages, so easy on the clarinet, are the most usual source of trouble to the violist.

Two other sets of pieces of medium difficulty, again by British composers, are *Four Pieces* by Alec Rowley, and *Four Pieces* by Thomas Dunhill. I find these two sets are more useful for teaching than for concert performance. Teachers owe a great debt to the modern English school of composers who have devoted so much of their time to supplying the requirements of the pupil in his second or third year. For advanced players looking for a brilliant show piece I recommend *Moto Perpetuo* by David Moule Evans. This is really difficult and very good practice. It is published by Joseph Williams who have several more pieces in their catalogue which may prove useful[2]. These include: *Romance in D flat*, Op. 9, by Ernest Walker, *Romance*, Op 72, by Hans Sitt; and *Caprice* by Walter Swanson.

Also difficult, but well worth the effort, is *Intrada* by Alan Richardson. You will enjoy working at this piece. It has an attractive Scottish touch about it. If it is a little too difficult try the same composer's *Sussex Lullaby*, surely one of the loveliest pieces in the repertoire. I have always enjoyed playing the *Six Studies in English Folk Song* by Vaughan Williams. They are not suitable for every audience, for they are serious, five out of the six are slow, but it is possible to make a selection. Numbers 5 and 6 are the most immediately attractive; none is very difficult technically.

There is an attractive set of light pieces: *A Mosaic in Ten Pieces* by Richard Walthew and published by Boosey & Hawkes. The fact that they are also written for clarinet is only noticeable here and there and gives rise to no great difficulties. The pieces are very short and make good teaching material for younger students. Although they are joined together in musical sequence, it is possible to play a selection in a separated group. Numbers 1, 4, 6 and 9 are the best. Boosey & Hawkes also publish a slow air calculated to show off the viola to its best advantage, the *Crepuscule by* Philip Sainton.

Many readers will remember the ballet *Nobilissima Visione* by Hindemith, produced in the summer of 1938 by the

Russian Ballet. Hindemith has extracted a portion of the score and made it into a very interesting viola solo–*Meditation*. This is powerful music, and I think you will eventually like it, but you want to get to know it really well before forming a definite opinion. The only real technical difficulty, the very high section in the middle, may be played an octave lower.

Besides these short pieces and suites there are a number of longer solos, lasting from five to ten minutes about which the player might care to know. One of the best is the *Introduction and Dance* by Joseph Jongen. This is a brilliant piece full of verve. I think you will prefer this to any other work on a similar scale I may include in this list. It is very well written for the instrument, all the technical writing making for effective results. Then there is a *Ballade* by Leo Weiner. It is an interesting though not very mature work and is not without an occasional dull patch. There are some very good ideas well worked out, and it is quite a pleasant work to listen to. There is also a *Romance, Scherzo and Finale* by Gabriel Grovlez. I have never greatly cared for this piece, but perhaps it is a personal dislike. I feel there are finer things more worthy of attention. We are lucky to have the *Legende* by Bax, which I may have mentioned previously. Written in this composer's familiar Celtic idiom it represents him at his best, and it is a good piece in a serious programme. It is also interesting to study for the development of tone colour.

The pupil should be encouraged to make his selection of pieces on broad lines. As regards the shorter solos it is best for him to make his own choice, for only then will he build up his own personal repertoire. Whereas his list of standard works is practically settled for him since there are so few viola masterpieces from which to choose, it is possible to have a certain variety in his shorter pieces, and that this personal repertoire should be encouraged is only too apparent when we notice how most violinists and pianists tend to play the same small group of works. When we further realise how much the repertoire of any solo instrument has been augmented in recent years by the addition of numberless arrangements, there is obviously plenty of scope for individuality—even for the viola player.

(Reprinted from the Strad Magazine, March 1941)

Short pieces arranged for the Viola

There are no hard and fast rules as to what is really good in music: but when some piece has for a considerable period of time enjoyed the appreciation and commendation of those most suited to judge, i.e., critics and performers, it may fairly be assumed that particular piece is good and therefore deserves to be known. There are countless reasons why what is universally recognised as good deserves to be known, and equally many reasons why people who are already fortunate in their knowledge should share this good fortune with such of their fellow citizens who have ears to appreciate the good things. Now, it may so happen that the piece of music in question may have been composed many years ago and written to be played on an instrument since forgotten or which fashion has rendered obsolete; or again, the piece may be of fairly recent composition, and being written in the popular idiom of the moment deserves to be known to as wide a public as quickly as possible.

Whatever the reason, it is frequently recognised that although a composer first thought of his piece for a particular instrument or in a particular setting, the musical public is often prepared to accept it in various forms and even thus prefer it.

The ethics of the subject must surely trouble the sensitive artist, but so much depends on circumstances; whether, for instance, it is better to know Beethoven's Ninth Symphony in a two-piano version than never to know it at all; or again, whether to tolerate the jazzed up versions of the classics on the strength that, at any rate, the tunes are good. It is like many other problems in art—a matter of taste, and where taste is concerned complete agreement is the exception. But avoiding extremes and coming in particular to that section of the musical public which has a conscience where the works of great composers are concerned, we find that the performance of arrangements within strictly defined limits is tolerated and almost encouraged. Thus many a lesser masterpiece is sometimes better known in its arranged form (e.g., Bach's *Air* on *the G string*) and indeed it is from among these smaller pieces that we find scope for a certain ingenuity which we hope the composer might condone and which at the same time might prove a valuable link between art and a wider public.

Few instruments have to rely on arrangements for their repertoire of short solos quite so much as the viola. I have already in previous articles dealt with a selection of the original short solos and here are some suggestions for adding to your repertoire by the use of arrangements.

Allow me to discuss these under two headings: (1) where the arrangement has already been made and published, and (2) where no viola versions exist but where little or no alteration to a violin or cello copy will suffice. This latter is not strictly an arrangement but an adaptation and where no new manuscript copy has to be made does not, I believe, infringe copyright.

Lionel Tertis, who has so far done more than any other player to lay the foundation for a viola repertoire, has himself re-arranged many of the existing violin arrangements. From the interesting series by Burmester he has re-arranged six pieces in the Schott edition, the Minuets by Haydn, Mozart and Beethoven being particularly attractive. From the same edition I should like to mention his version of the *Londonderry Air* one of the best known arrangements and one which the player can make easy or difficult, according to his choice of fingering. Another of his most popular arrangements and one within the reach of all but first year students is his version of the Delius *Serenade from Hassan*. A haunting tune in a lovely setting—how intriguing these changing harmonies will be to young students coming up against the modern idiom for the first time!

A comprehensive view of all that Lionel Tertis has done in this direction is difficult as his arrangements have been published by so many different firms. I cannot possibly mention all of them but here are some others which deserve attention. First is the lovely *Aria* by Porpora—surely one of the most expressive melodies from this period of music and incidentally a fine study for tone production. In a lighter style is the *Serenade in A* by Gabriel Pierné, not great music but just the thing for certain occasions. Tertis has made many transcriptions of the works of Delius (readers will remember his viola version of the violin sonatas which I mentioned earlier), and here are two of the cello works—*Elegy* and *Caprice*. The latter is a very slight piece but the *Elegy* is finer. Neither, perhaps, represent Delius at his very best. A selection from these arrangements will prove a convenient nucleus from which to build up a representative collection of small pieces.

Every publisher now has in his catalogue a reasonably varied number of viola arrangements usually found in album form. Some of these albums I have previously mentioned in connection with first-year pieces. They invariably consist of more or less familiar selections from the classics, but not all of them are exclusively devoted to easy pieces. Some are graded according to difficulty, the later volumes often including pieces graded as 'moderately difficult' to 'very difficult,' and it is always advisable to have several of these albums in your library which you can consult from time to time. It is not to be expected that the arrangements to be found here will be in the nature of the artistic creations, or paraphrases to which Kreisler and Heifetz have accustomed us in recent years. They are straightforward transcriptions, with the further advantage of a simple piano part—a very necessary convenience where the capabilities of the accompanist are quite unknown.

Paul Klengel has been more industrious and successful in making these collections. He has selected and edited three different volumes of classical pieces for both the Peters and Breitkopf editions. The same editor has three further volumes of medium difficulty in the Schott edition called *Recital pieces*, ranging from Bach and Beethoven to modern pieces by Elgar and Sibelius — and not forgetting Mr Klengel himself! Alfred Moffatt is also celebrated in the same way for several series of violin arrangements, many of them quite new discoveries and not likely to be found in other collections. Schott publishes an excellent album containing twelve of these pieces in re-edited form for the viola; Augener, too, have a similar album. In addition, Schott offers us five excellent volumes of classical pieces selected and edited by Ries. Other albums in the Augener edition are best suited for beginners only.

Taking it altogether the viola player, of whatever degree of accomplishment, is fairly well catered for in these albums, and they represent a convenient and comprehensive source of supply alike for both teacher and performer.

Let me now give you a further selection of pieces that have interested me. The popular Debussy pieces, *Reverie* and *Clair de Lune*, originally for piano, have been arranged by Roelens; they are effective and not too difficult. There is, too, an *Aria* by Ibert, not so immediately attractive but nevertheless worthy of consideration. Of *Three Romances* by Schumann, that in A, No. 2, is quite the best. Kreisler made a violin arrangement of this piece which was very popular, and viola players will find their version equally acceptable. The two celebrated pieces by Faure, *Berceuse* and *Elegy*, are also published for viola. They are too well known to need further recommendation.

A recent addition which deserves to have a good following is the Bach Choral prelude, *O Man Thy Heavy Sin Bewail*, arranged by Lionel Salter and published by Joseph Williams. I have myself edited and fingered the viola part, which readily lends itself to interesting effects of tonal contrasts. In collaboration with Alan Richardson I have transcribed two pieces from the unaccompanied violin works of Bach—the *Prelude and Gavotte from* the E major partita. In the viola version they are transposed to A and supplied with original piano accompaniments. These movements, difficult in the original for violin, are correspondingly more difficult for viola. They will be found specially useful to players who first knew them as violin pieces and later became viola players. They are published by the Oxford University Press, who also publish my arrangement of *Two Folk Tunes*, by William Alwyn. Cellists know these as very attractive pieces and I hope viola players will find them equally useful.

On the whole it is better to avoid re–arrangements of pieces already very celebrated for another instrument, although this is not always possible. The violin has naturally first claim to many of these arrangements, especially where it helped in the first place to make the original piece popular. Thus, many know the *Brahms Hungarian Dances* only in the Joachim edition for violin and piano; many also know such pieces as Dvorak's *Humoresque*, Handel's *Largo*, Brahms' *Waltz in A*, Beethoven's *Minuet in G*, etc., only as violin solos. It need hardly be said that it is possible to build up a considerable viola repertoire without having to encroach on any of the celebrated violin transcriptions. As in his selection of viola solos the student should be encouraged by his teacher to make his own repertoire of arrangements; he can still further augment the list by his own personal selection from the second heading I mentioned earlier in the article by using an existing violin or cello arrangement which requires little or no alteration for it to be possible on the viola. I can best illustrate this by mentioning one or two popular examples: Bach, *Air on the G string*; Kreisler, *Chanson Louis XIII* and *Pavane*; Rachmaninov, *Vocalise*; Martini, *Arietta*; Sibelius, *Solitary Song* (where the viola has the advantage, the violin G string having to be tuned down to get the low F) For other works requiring only slight alteration, try *Sicilienne* by Paradies, *Cradle Song* by Tor Aulin, *Cradle Song* by Hugo Wolf, and *Rondino* by Beethoven–Kreisler.

More enterprising viola players will perform violin pieces transposed down a fifth, which means that the piece can be played with the same violin fingering on the corresponding viola strings. The accompaniment will also have to be transposed and even on occasions redistributed, but the player must note that in copyright works the permission of the publisher has to be obtained before the arrangement is made. Try for a start such pieces as the *Tambourin* by Gossec, and the *Allegro* by Piocco.

The reader will now see how wide and varied is the music the viola player can draw on for both his concert repertoire and teaching material. Arrangements specially made for the viola are naturally the most satisfactory, but until their number has been greatly added to, the viola player will still have to use his imagination and ingenuity in making his repertoire sufficiently comprehensive to meet every occasion.

(Reprinted from the Strad Magazine, June 1947)

Viola Duets

In the course of these articles I have covered most of the viola repertoire. There is still, however, one section at which I have only hinted, and it might be as well if I drew the viola enthusiast's attention towards it in this, my concluding article. I refer to viola duets with an instrument other than the piano. It is part of the repertoire about which very little is known. Let me hasten to add that it is not a very important section, since it contains few masterpieces; yet it has a certain interest for various reasons, not all of them connected with public performance.

The most usual form is the duet for violin and viola. Now this is useful principally for teachers and students. It is helpful where the student has no piano and realises the benefits to be derived from playing with another instrument. It is in many ways ensemble playing in its simplest form and, indeed, might well be the student's first approach to chamber music playing. The blending of two stringed instruments is often easier for the young student to assimilate than the sometimes disconcerting volume of the pianoforte. The addition by a teacher of a viola part to a dry technical study often works wonders in stimulating the pupil to fresh efforts and may even help him to appreciate the rhythmic and harmonic foundations. There are countless occasions which any teacher of experience can relate where the idea has proved its worth.

Not many people, however, realise the useful function that violin and viola duets can play on the concert platform. Briefly, they can sometimes supply a welcome relief by giving a change of colour. A duet between two long and musically heavy string quartets often restores just the right balance to a programme. For demonstrating at children's concerts both the similarity and the contrast between the violin and the viola, a short duet movement is just the thing to appeal to the child's imagination. Lastly, strange to relate, several works can claim an occasional performance purely because of their own musical worth!

The use of two violins was favoured by the early violin composers, i.e., from Corelli up to, and including Bach and Handel—it was a long time before the viola could establish a claim. Yet one often feels that the contrasting tone of the viola would have clarified many a passage written in canon, or added a new significance to a repeated tune. That the later violin teachers appreciated how useful the contrasting tone could be in throwing the first violin into relief is shown by the number of times they made use of the violin with viola accompaniment. Thus Reis, Baillot, Rode, Kreutzer, Spohr, Beriot, Dancla, Mazas; and later, David and Dont, all either wrote original duets or added a viola accompaniment to their celebrated books of studies and caprices. Even Paganini wrote a sonata for violin solo to which he later added a viola accompaniment. This is published by Schott.

One composer, undistinguished in many ways, who has yet given many amateurs some very pleasurable hours is Pleyel. He understood the requirements of the less advanced player to perfection and wrote expressly for him, technical difficulties being reduced to suit all standards of proficiency. He wrote *Three Duets, Op.* 69 and if you are lucky you may still get a copy in the Peters or Litolff Editions. In a similar category are some duets by Kalliwoda and three duets by Bruni, whose viola tutor and studies I have previously mentioned.

Michael Haydn, brother to the famous Joseph, was one of the first to write for violin and viola. He wrote four sonatas, published in two books by Breitkopf. As a composer he was truly modest, refusing to have anything published during his lifetime. Yet we know from various sources that he was much thought of by Schubert and more especially by Mozart. Mozart's friendship was the principal factor in a very odd incident. Once when Haydn was ill, so the story goes, Mozart visited him and as a token of his esteem actually wrote two duets for violin and viola, supposed to be in imitation of Haydn's style. These two duets were even published and circulated as Haydn's own compositions, and it was only later, as they became better known, that the public realised the true composer was Mozart. To this incident we owe the composition of the two principal works in this branch of our repertoire.

The duets are two full–length works in sonata form, each having three movements. The first, in G, is more brilliant and technically showy. The second, in B flat, however, has the better music. The various difficult problems inherent in writing sonatas for, in the main, two parts only, seem to have stimulated Mozart to some of his finest work. The variety of colour and texture combined with the sonority of sound, is truly amazing. The part writing is practically confined to two parts throughout, the principal exception being the slow movement of the second duet where the viola supplies the accompaniment to the violin melody by playing in double stops. The last movement of this duet, which is in variation form, is one of the most astonishing feats of technical power combined with musical worth that Mozart has ever given us. The duets are published in various editions and are also recorded by Decca.

The duet by Spohr is almost the only other original work in the classical repertoire worthy of performance. The name of Spohr appears so infrequently in our concert programmes that it is difficult for us to realise that, in his day, Spohr was actually considered to be the equal of Beethoven! A sickly chromaticism in the harmony and the realisation that his themes were not so profound after all, have sounded the death knell of Spohr's popularity. His *Last Judgement* and some violin works are the only things which still remain, his violin concerto *Vocal Scena* being a really fine work. Doubtless his duets for two violins are still played in private and this duet, Op. 13, for violin and viola, is worth an occasional performance. It is an early work and in some ways not so exciting as his violin duets. Do not be misled in the first movement by the marking 'Allegro Moderato' in 3/4. The quaver is really the beat, as you will quickly find out in the course of the first few lines. So, too, in the last movement, a triplet passage on the second page will give you the clue to the tempo. There are some rather fine moments in the slow movement and, indeed, Spohr gets some truly amazing effects when both instruments are playing in double stopping; the effect is almost that of a string quartet.

Before leaving the classical repertoire, I should like to mention the strange viola and cello duet by Beethoven. The idea of a viola and cello playing a duet sounds like a joke, and so indeed it is, for its full title is *Duet with an obbligato for two eye glasses!* Apparently Beethoven wrote for two of his keen amateur musical friends who, even with spectacles, were still short sighted. In the Peters edition there are some impossible turns which added still further to the fun when the duet was used some time ago as the basis of a comic item on the Variety stage! The music, which is in sonata form, can, however, be treated seriously, and as such is pleasant though not very distinguished Beethoven. Both parts, especially the cello, have very awkward moments, and we cannot help but feel that most of the humour of the situation was enjoyed by Beethoven at his friends' expense.

From the modern repertoire there is a duet by Ernst Toch. This is very modern in idiom and will appeal only to those readers who have both the technique and the time to sort it out, for it is really difficult. I have not yet heard a public performance. Two copies (in score) are necessary for performance, and it is published by Schott.Of the modern English works I have performed, here are three, none of which, unfortunately, is published. One by Arnold Cooke, an early work, shows the influence of Hindemith. A *Fantasy Sonata* which William Alwyn wrote for me, is more English in character. This has a rhapsodic introduction followed by a very clever theme and variations. There is some exceedingly effective writing for both instruments. Two short pieces, *The Lonely Moor* and *Jig*, by Spain–Dunk, are welcome additions to the lighter side of the repertoire. They were recently broadcast. The possibility of publishing these works at the present time is very remote, but I hope that later some enterprising publisher will include them in his catalogue.

Of arrangements, there are twelve quite easy and interesting pieces by Mozart, originally for basset–horns. The Two–part Inventions by Bach are an obvious choice and David has arranged four of them for Breitkopf. He has also arranged some similar pieces by Bach—*Four Duets*, which are little known even in their original version for clavichord. They are fine music and, like much of Bach, sound quite at home in the arranged form, though most people will quarrel with David's tempi and also with his marks of expression!

Two pieces, half arrangement, half original work. are the *Passacaglia* and the *Sarabande with Variations* by Handel–Halvorsen. They will surely have a permanent place in the repertoire. Halvorsen, a Norwegian virtuoso violinist, writes brilliantly and effectively for the instruments, each of which has ample opportunity for technical display. The *Passacaglia is* the better known and the more immediately attractive of the two. I should like to make it clear that all these duets I have mentioned are complete in themselves and have no piano accompaniment.

I can add no further works without embarking on a discussion of chamber music, a field which can hardly be called viola repertoire! So, in coming to the end, I find the list of works included is very long—much longer than most people would have thought possible—and, until I had actually catalogued it, much more comprehensive than I had imagined. The viola enthusiast who contemplates mastering this repertoire has years of hard work in front of him and many moments of great joy, for the repertoire has so many real masterpieces and is now so important that the future of the viola as a solo instrument is assured.

(Reprinted from the Strad Magazine, 1947)

Appendix I1

Arrangements

There is a great antipathy towards accepting works arranged for performance on instruments other than those visualised by the composer. Yet, at the same time, we accept certain kinds of arrangements without perhaps fully realising what we are about. Bach wrote most of his keyboard works for the harpsichord, or even the clavichord; so did Mozart. Yet we play them on the piano. It is even recorded that Mozart himself played his compositions in a style only suited to the harpsichord and quite ungrateful to the piano.

Great composers made arrangements of their own and other people's music. We have only to recall Bach's attitude to some of Vivaldi's works and, coming nearer home, how Brahms made his clarinet sonatas available for viola players. And what are we to do about such a popular work as Schubert's 'Arpeggione' sonata? There were only two such arpeggione instruments in Schubert's time, and modern examples are few and far between. Is such a work to be left languishing on the shelf simply because some people object to arrangements?

When we consider the wealth of music written for the piano or for the violin and realise that even these instruments are happy to accept arrangements, what have we to say for an instrument like the viola with a minute repertoire of worthwhile original works? I am aware that scholars and players have diligently searched and discovered and published many original works for viola which have for many years lain forgotten. I am also aware that many composers in this century have written new works specially for the viola. But when we contemplate the result of all this hard endeavour, the repertoire of really worthwhile works still remains small. Like many a viola player I have a huge cupboard full of viola music which has had its day, and now collects the dust, unwanted and unplayed.

We are going through a period when the works of great composers are being reverently re-edited. We go one step further and have these works recorded on instruments such as were available to the composer when he wrote the work, and we even endeavour to go one step further still and try to play these instruments in a style suitable to the period. This is fine. All of us can learn from this diligent research. But this is for the purist, and not at all suitable for the bread-and-butter concert, where music lovers congregate to hear music for the love of music as they are accustomed to hear it. Not everyone wishes to have a lecture in history. We cannot condemn if a listener wants to bring twentieth century ears and understanding to a concert.

As in all things there is the question of taste. An arrangement can be a simple transference or an elaborate transcription. We read the Bible, we read Dante, we read Omar Khayyam in translation, without bothering overmuch about the original. We leave that to the scholar. More accurate, more modern translations of these works don't necessarily increase our love and respect for these masterpieces. It is a matter of opinion how far you can go in adapting the original to its new form. Beethoven was very outspoken — he was against transplanting keyboard pieces to stringed instruments; only Mozart and Haydn, he averred, were competent at such transcriptions. But he did in fact sometimes sanction transcriptions of his own works, and even made some himself—e.g. the String Quartet in F is from the Piano Sonata in E, op. 14, no. 1 but Beethoven usually left it to others to make arrangements of his works, he merely revised and corrected the manuscripts before publication. The Serenade for String Trio, op. 8, is a case in point. The arrangement for viola and piano is even given a new opus number—Notturno, op. 42.

It is perhaps in teaching material that we find arrangements for the viola so helpful. Pieces and studies will always be in short supply, and think of the joy of a young instrumentalist when he learns and plays some music by a great composer. I think we must keep an open mind in relation to arrangements, and not become too precious in our choice of what we play. It should be our endeavour to see that whatever we do play is good, worthwhile music, and if it is backed up by the personality of a good composer, so much the better.

APPENDIX 3

ARRANGEMENTS, TRANSCRIPTIONS AND EDITIONS

Composer	Title	Publisher
Viola Solo		
Arnell, Richard (1917-	Partita	Hinrichsen (1961)
Bach, Johann Sebastian) (1685- 1750)	Album: Baroque Pieces for Viola	OUP (1986)
	Chaconne	MS
	Six Suites for Viola (originally for cello)	Chester (1951 & 1990)
	Solo Sonatas & Partitas (violin)	Hinrichsen
		Peters
	Sonata no.1 & Partita no.1 BWV 1001 & 1002	Peters (1961)
	Toccata & Fugue in D minor	MS
Forbes, Watson	A Book of Daily Exercises for Viola Players	OUP (1949)
	Exercises for Viola Players:	Associated Board
	Grade 2	Associated Board
	Grade 3	Associated Board
	Grade 4	Associated Board
	Grade 5	Associated Board
	A First Book of Scales & Arpeggios for Viola Players	OUP (1951)
	A Second Book of Scales & Arpeggios for Viola Players	OUP (1951)
	A Third Book of Scales & Arpeggios for Viola Players	OUP (1954)
	New Editions edited by John White:	
	A First Book of Scales & Arpeggios for Viola Players	Corda Publications (1993)

	A Second Book of Scales & Arpeggios for Viola Players	(1993)
	A Third Book of Scales & Arpeggios for Viola Players	(1993/94)
	A Book of Daily Exercises for Viola Players	(1993/94)
Paganini, Niccolo (1782-1840)	Caprice Op 1 no.14 (freely arranged as a study in double-stopping)	MS
Viola & Piano		
Albeniz, Isaac (1860-1909)	Tango (from Espana Op 165 no.2)	OUP (1962)
Alwyn, William (1905-1985)	Two Folk Tunes	OUP
	Three Negro Spirituals (arranged Alwyn):	MS
	(a) I'll hear the trumpet sound	
	(b) I'm travelling to the grave	
	(c) Didn't my Lord deliver Daniel?	
Arne, Thomas (1710-1778)	Sonata in B flat (Harold Craxton) * (originally for harpsichord)	OUP (1950)
Bach, Johann Sebastian (1685- 1750)	Andante (Alec Robertson) *	Curwen
	Choral Prelude - O Man thy Heavy Sin Bewail (Lionel Salter) *	Joseph Williams
	Gavotte in A (Violin Partita no.3) BWV 1006 (Alan Richardson) *	OUP (1939)
	Jesu, Joy of Man's Desiring	OUP (1949)
	Prelude in A (Violin Partita no.3) BWV 1006 (Alan Richardson) *	OUP (1939)
	Sheep May Safely Graze	OUP (1939)
	Sleepers, Wake! (William Alwyn) *	OUP (1946)
	Sonata no.1 in E flat (harpsichord/organ)	MS
	Sonata no.2 in C minor (harpsichord/organ)	MS
	Sonata no.3 in D minor (harpsichord/organ)	MS

Bach J.S. (cont)	Sonata no.4 in E minor (harpsichord/organ)	MS
	Sonata no.5 in C (harpsichord/organ)	MS
	Sonata no.6 in G (harpsichord/organ)	MS
	Sonata in E minor (flute no.1)	MS
	Sonata in E flat (flute no.2)	MS
	Sonata in F (violin) BWV 1022	Peters (1958)
	Three Choral Preludes:	OUP (1945)
	(a) Lord Jesus Christ, Be Present Now	
	(b) Come, Redeemer of our Race	
	(c) All Glory be to God on High	
	(Alan Richardson) *	
	Three Sonatas (viola da gamba) BWV1027 - 1029	Peters (1951)
Beethoven, Ludwig van (1770-1827)	Alla Polacca (Serenade Op 8)	OUP (1951)
	Country Dances (Alan Richardson) *	OUP (1949)
	Romances Op 40 &Op 50 (violin)	Stainer & Bell
	Rondo in G (Wo 041)	Schott (1957)
	7 Variations in E flat on Mozart's 'Bei Mannern, welche Liebe fuhlen (cello) from 'Magic Flute' (Wo 046)	Peters (1961)
	Sonata Movement	Novello
	Sonata no.2 Op 5 no.2 (cello)	Stainer & Bell
	Sonata no.3 in A major Op 69 (cello)	Stainer & Bell
	Sonata in F Op 24 'Spring' (violin)	Peters (1960)
	SonatasOp 12 nos.1,2 & 3 (violin)	Stainer & Bell

Composer	Work	Publisher
Beethoven (cont)	Variations on Mozart's 'Ein Madchen oder Weibchen' Op 66 (cello)	Peters
Berkeley, Sir Lennox (1903-1989)	Sonata in D minor Op 22 (1945)	Chester (1949)
Bliss, Sir Arthur (1891 -1975)	Intermezzo (piano quartet) 1915	OUP (1950)
Boyce, William (1710-1779)	Tempo di Gavotta (Harold Craxton) *	OUP (1948)
Brahms, Johannes (1833-1897)	Sonata in A Op 100 (violin)	Stainer & Bell
	Sonata in E flat Op 120 no.2 (clarinet)	Stainer & Bell
	Sonata in F minor Op 120 no.1 (clarinet)	Stainer & Bell (1985)
	Sonata in G Op 78 (violin)	Stainer & Bell
	Sonata Movement (violin) (Sonatensatz) Scherzo (1853)	Stainer & Bell (1983)
	Two Hungarian Dances nos.1 & 3	Hinrichsen (1961)
Corelli, Arcangelo (1653-1713)	Sonata da Camera Op 1 no.8 (Alan Richardson) *	OUP (1948)
Couperin, Francois (1668- 1733)	Suite: Concerts Royaux (Alan Richardson) *	OUP (1947)
Dvorak, Antonin (1841 -1904)	Bagatelle Op 47 no.3	Hinrichsen (1960)
	Mazurka Op 49	MS
	Sonatina Op 100 (violin)	Stainer & Bell
	Three Slavonic Dances	MS

Composer	Work	Publisher
Elgar, Sir Edward (1857-1934)	La Capricieuse Salut d'Amour	MS MS
Faure, Gabriel (1845-1924)	Sonata no.1 (violin)	Stainer & Bell
Ferguson, Howard (1908-	Five Irish FolkTunes	OUP (1944)
Forbes, Sebastian (1941 -	Two Scottish FolkSongs	MS
Forbes Watson	Album Baroque Pieces for Viola	OUP (1986)
	Album A Book of Classical Pieces	OUP
	Album A Second Book of Classical Pieces	OUP (1958)
	Album Chester Music for Viola & Piano	Chester (1989)
	Album Classical & Romantic Pieces	OUP (1974)
	Album A First Year Classical Album	OUP (1955)
	Album A Second Year Classical Album	OUP (1960)
	Album Popular Pieces	OUP (1980)
	Album Tunes & Dances (9 pieces)	OUP (1982)
	Albums Four Albums of Graded Pieces	MS
Forbes, Watson & Richardson, Alan	'Two Scottish Tunes' * (a) The Lea Rig (b) Whaur the Gadie Rins	OUP (1952)
Franck, Cesar (1822-1890)	Sonata in A (violin)	Stainer & Bell

Composer	Work	Publisher
Fulton, Norman (1909-1980)	Introduction, Air & Reel	OUP (1951)
	Sonata da Camera (1945)	Chester (1952)
Gow, David (1924-1993)	Nocturne & Capriccio Op 31	Augener (1957)
Greenwood, John (1889-1975)	Sonata	MS
	Viola Concerto	MS
Grieg, Edvard (1843-1907)	To the Spring Op 47 no.6	OUP
Handel, George Frideric (1685-1759)	Arrival of the Queen of Sheba	OUP (1963)
	Sonata in A (violin) Op 1 no.15 (Alan Richardson) *	OUP (1943)
	Sonata in B flat	Viola World. USA (1993)
	Sonata in G Op 1 no.13	OUP (1986)
Harrison, Pamela (1915-1990)	Sonata	MS
Haydn, Franz Joseph (1732-1809)	Adagio (from String Quartet Op 20 no.5)	OUP (1953)
Ilynsky, Alexander (1859-1919)	Berceuse	Chester (1956)
Jacobsen, Maurice (1896-1976)	Berceuse	OUP (1946)
Leigh, Walter (1905-1942)	Sonatina (1932)	MS

Leighton, Kenneth (1929-1988)	Fantasia on the name BACH Op 29 (1955)	Novello (1957)
McEwen, Sir John B. (1868-1948)	Sonata (1939-41) (Scottish Music Archive)	MS
Medtner, Nicholas (1880-1951)	Fairy Tale Op 51 no.3	Zimmerman
Mendelssohn, Felix (1809-1847)	Sonata no.1 Op 45 (cello)	Stainer & Bell
	Sonata in D (violin) (Menuhin)	MS
	Song without Words (cello)	MS
	Two Songs without Words	Chester
Moore, John (1898-	Scottish Song (Turn ye to me)	OUP (1949)
Mozart, Wolfgang Amadeus (175u-1791)	Adagio K261 & Rondo K373 (Alan Richardson) *	OUP (1952)
	Minuet in C (from Divertimento no.2 K229)	Schott (1957)
	Sonata in C K296 (violin)	Stainer & Bell
	Sonata in E minor K304 (violin)	Peters (1963)
	Sonata in F K377 (violin)	Stainer & Bell
	Sonata in G K301 (violin)	Stainer & Bell
Murrill, Herbert (1909-1952)	Sarabande	OUP (1953)
Nardini, Pietro (1722-1793)	Concerto no.10 in G minor (Alan Richardson) *	OUP (1950)

		MS
Orr, Robin (1909-	Sicilienne and Chaconne (1949) (on hire from Hinrichsen)	
Paganini, Niccolo (1782-1840)	Sonata (1946/47) Sonata (new edition) Moto PerpetuoOp 11 Sonata No 12 (Alan Richardson) *	OUP (1949) Anglo-American Music Publishers (1981) OUP (1952) Augener (1960) Stainer & Bell
Paradies, Pietro Domenico (1707-1791)	Two Caprices no.13 & no.20 (Alan Richardson) * Toccata in C	Hinrichsen (1953) OUP (1957)
Purcell, Henry (1659-1695)	Bourree & Hornpipe Sonata in G minor (Alan Richardson) *	Chester (1956) OUP (1946)
Rameau, Jean Philippe (1683-1764)	Suite of Three Dances (Alan Richardson) *	OUP (1943)
Rawsthorne, Alan (1905-1971)	Sonata (1937)	OUP (1955)
Rebikov, Vladimir (1866-1920)	Berceuse & Dance	Chester (1956)
Richardson, Alan (1904-1978)	Autumn Sketches Intrada Sonata Op 21 Sussex Lullaby	OUP (1949) OUP (1939) Augener (1955) OUP (1938)

Composer	Work	Publisher
Schubert, Franz (1797-1828)	Reverie (Sonata in A Op 120) Sonata in A DV821 'Arpeggione' (viola part only)	OUP (1963) Joseph Williams (1940)
	Sonata Movement (Sonatensatz) D471 Three Sonatinas	Stainer & Bell (1960) Stainer & Bell (1957) Augener
Tartini, Guiseppe (1692-1770)	Sonata in C minor Op 1 no.10 (Alan Richardson) *	OUP (1954)
Tchaikovsky, Peter Ilich (1840-1893)	Barcarolle Op 37a no.6 Chanson Triste Op 40 no.2 Chanson Italienne Op 39a no.15	Chester (1958) Chester (1958) Chester (1958)
Telemann, Georg Philipp (1681-1767)	Suite in D (Bergmann)	Schott (1952)
Vaughan Williams, Ralph (1872-1958)	Fantasia on 'Greensleeves'	OUP (1947)
Vivaldi, Antonio (1678-1741)	Concerto in A minor (violin)	MS
Weber, Carl Maria von (1786-1826)	March Op 3 no.5 Serenata Op 3 no.1	Roberton Schott (1958)
Wieniawski, Henri (1835-1880)	Two Caprices (Alan Richardson) * (a) Alla Saltarella Op 10 no.5 (b) Alla Tarantella Op 18 no.4	Hinrichsen (1953)

Two Violas & Piano

Bach, Johann Sebastian (1685- 1750)

Brandenburg Concerto no.6 — Hinrichsen (1962)

Handel, George Frideric (1685-1759)

Arrival of the Queen of Sheba — OUP (1963)

Violin Solo

Bach, Johann Sebastian (1685-1750)

Baroque Pieces for Violin (16 Dance Movements from Solo Cello Suites) — OUP (1986)

Forbes, Watson

Scales & Arpeggios Book 1 (Grades 1-5) (Gertrude Collins) — Associated Board

Scales & Arpeggios Book 2 (Grades 6-8) (Gertrude Collins) — Associated Board

Exercises for Violinists Grade 1
Exercises for Violinists Grade 2
Exercises for Violinists Grade 3
Exercises for Violinists Grade 4
Exercises for Violinists Grade 5 — Associated Board

Two Violins

Forbes, Watson

Album Bach Duets for 2 Violins — OUP
Album Duets for 2 Violins Book 1 — Chester
Album Duets for 2 Violins Book 2 — Chester
Album Handel Duets for 2 Violins — OUP

Two Violins & Piano

Forbes, Watson — Album Duets for 2 Violins & Piano — OUP

Handel, George Frideric (1685-1759) — Arrival of the Queen of Sheba, 2 violins & piano — OUP (1963)

Duets for Violin & Viola

Bach, Johann Sebastian (1685-1750) — Two Canons from the Art of Fugue — Peters

Handel, George Frideric (1685-1759) — Arrival of the Queen of Sheba (with piano) — OUP (1963)

Duets for Violin & Viola — MS

Violin & Cello

Bach, Johann Sebastian (1685-1750) — Two Canons from the Art of Fugue — MS

Handel, George Frideric (1685-1759) — Duets for Violin & Cello — MS

Violin & Piano

Albeniz, Isaac (1860-1909) — Tango — OUP (1962)

Alwyn, William (1905-1985) — Two Folk Tunes — OUP

Composer	Work	Publisher
Bach, Johann Sebastian (1685-1750)	Sheep may safely graze	OUP (1946)
Brahms, Johannes (1833-1897)	Sonata Movement (Sonatensatz) Scherzo (1853)	Stainer & Bell (1983)
Dvorak, Antonin (1841 -1904)	Bagatelle Op 47 no.3	Hinrichsen
Forbes, Watson	Album A First Book of Classical & Romantic Pieces	OUP (1962)
	Album A Second Book of Classical & Romantic Pieces	OUP (1962)
	Album A Third Book of Classical & Romantic Pieces	OUP (1962)
	Album A Fourth Book of Classical & Romantic Pieces	OUP (1962)
	Album Popular Pieces	OUP
	Album Scottish Airs, Strathspeys & Reels, 2 books	MS
	Album Slow Movements (simplified) from the concertos of Bruch, Mendelssohn & Tchaikovsky	Peters
	Album Tunes & Dances (9 pieces)	OUP (1982)
Grieg, Edvard (1843-1907)	To the Spring	OUP
Handel, George Frideric (1685-1759)	Arrival of the Queen of Sheba	OUP (1963)
	Rondeau (from Sonata in E minor Op 5 no.3) 'First Violin'	Associated Board
Haydn, Franz Joseph (1732-1809)	Adagio (from String Quartet Op 20 no.5)	OUP

Ilynsky, Alexander (1859-1919)	Berceuse	Chester (1956)
Murrill, Herbert (1909-1952)	Sarabande	OUP (1953)
Schubert, Franz (1797-1828)	Reverie Sonata Movement (Sonatensatz) D471	OUP Stainer & Bell (1960)
Tchaikovsky, Peter Ilich (1840-1893)	Barcarolle Op 37a no.6	Chester (1958)
Weber, Carl Maria von (1786-1826)	March Op 3 no.5	Roberton

Cello Solo

Forbes, Watson	Scales & Arpeggios (Harvey Phillips)* Gradesl -5 Grades 6-8	Associated Board Associated Board

Cello & Piano

Bach, Johann Sebastian (1685-1750)	Sheep may safely graze Sonata in F (violin)	OUP (1946) Peters
Boyce, William (1710-1779)	Tempo di Gavotta (Harold Craxton)*	OUP (1948)
Brahms, Johannes (1833-1897)	Sonata Movement (Sonatensatz) Scherzo (1853)	Stainer & Bell (1983)

Forbes, Watson	Album A Book of Classical & Romantic Pieces	OUP (1973)
	Album A Second Book of Classical & Romantic Pieces	OUP
	Album Easy Classics for Cello	OUP (1969)
	Album A First Year Classical Album	OUP (1955)
	Album A Second Year Classical Album	OUP (1960)
	Album Popular Pieces	OUP (1982)
Grieg, Edvard (1843-1907)	Air from the Holberg Suite	OUP
Haydn, Franz Joseph (1732-1809)	Two Minuets (String Quartets)	OUP
Mozart, Wolfgang Amadeus (1756-1791)	Minuet in C	Schott
Murrill, Herbert (1909-1952)	Sarabande	OUP (1953)
Schubert, Franz (1797-1828)	Reverie	OUP (1963)
	Sonata Movement (Sonatensatz) D471	Stainer & Bell (1960)
Vaughan Williams, Ralph (1872-1958)	Fantasia on 'Greensleeves'	OUP (1947)
Weber, Carl Maria von (1786-1826)	March Op 3 no.5	Roberton

Descant Recorders & Piano

Forbes, Watson	Album	A Dvorak Suite for 2 Recorders & Piano	OUP
	Album	A Grieg Suite	OUP

Flute & Piano

Forbes, Watson	Album	Classical & Romantic Pieces Book 1	OUP
		Classical & Romantic Pieces Book 2	OUP

Flute & Clarinet

Forbes, Watson	Album	17 Short Duets from Three Centuries (Alan Frank)*	OUP

Oboe & Piano

Forbes, Watson	Album	Classical & Romantic Pieces Book 1	OUP (1987)
		Classical & Romantic Pieces Book 2	OUP

Two Clarinets

Forbes, Watson	Album	A Collection of Classical Pieces arranged for two clarinets (Alan Frank)*	
		Book 1	OUP (1962)
		Book 2	OUP (1962)

Mozart, Wolfgang Amadeus (1756-1791)	12 Duets	MS

Clarinet & Piano

Forbes, Watson

Album	A Beethoven Suite (Alan Frank)*	OUP
Album	A Brahms Suite (Alan Frank)*	OUP
Album	Classical & Romantic Pieces Book 1 (Alan Frank)*	OUP (1975)
	Classical & Romantic Pieces Book 2	OUP (1975)
Album	Easy Classics (Alan Frank)*	OUP
Album	A Mozart Suite (Alan Frank)*	OUP
Album	Tunes & Dances Book 1 (Alan Frank)*	OUP
	Tunes & Dances Book 2	OUP

Bassoon & Piano

Forbes, Watson

Album	A Book of Classical & Romantic Pieces Book 1	OUP (1977)
	A Book of Classical & Romantic Pieces Book 2	OUP (1977)

Horn & Piano

Forbes, Watson

Album	A Book of Classical & Romantic Pieces Book 2	OUP
	A Book of Classical & Romantic Pieces Book 3	

Trumpet in B flat & Piano

Forbes, Watson

Album	A Book of Classical Pieces Book 2	OUP
	A Book of Classical Pieces Book 3	

String Trios

Bach, Johann Sebastian
(1685- 1750)

2 Fugas (Contrapunctus 8 & 13) Art of Fugue	Peters
Trio Sonata No 2 in C minor	Peters

| Schubert, Franz (1797-1828) | Trio in B flat | Peters |
| | Trio in B flat (2 violins & cello) | Peters |

String Quartets

Forbes, Watson	Album	Easy String Quartets Book 1	Chester
		Easy String Quartets Book 2	
		Easy String Quartets Book 3	
		Playing for Pleasure	
		Mozart Rondo	Hinrichsen
		Mozart Andantino Grazioso	
Bach, Johann Sebastian (1685-1750)	Art of Fugue for vln, vla, cello, 2nd cello (or viola da gamba) (1944)	MS
	Five Fugues (Book 2 nos. 2,7,9,8,5) (1950)	MS
Borodin, Alexander (1 833-1887)	Nocturne (2nd String Quartet)	Hinrichsen

Piano Quintet

| Beethoven, Ludwig van (1770-1827) | Rondeau in B flat major (Alexander Feinland)* | Hinrichsen (1961) |

String Orchestra

| Bach, Johann Sebastian (1685-1750) | Ricercare (from the Musical Offering) | MS |
| Gay, John (1685-1732) | Beggar my Neighbour | Chester |

Handel, George Frideric (1685-1759)	Arrival of the Queen of Sheba	MS
Playstrings	Handel in Miniature	Chester
Playstrings	Mozart in Miniature (moderately easy)	Chester
Playstrings	Purcell in Miniature	Chester
Purcell, Henry (1659-1695)	Chacony	MS

Compilation

Chamber Music	Catalogue of chamber music compiled and selected by Watson Forbes for The National Federation of Music Societies	(1965)

NB: * = co-editors with Watson Forbes.